# AQA Unit 2 — Growing As a Business

## Section Six — The Business Organisation

## Section Seven — Marketing 2

## Section Eight — Finance 2

## Section Nine — People in Business 2

## Section Ten — Operations Management 2

## Assessment Tips

Published by CGP

*Editors:*
Katie Braid
Helena Hayes
Andy Park
David Ryan
Michael Southorn
Katherine Stewart
Andrew Wright

*Contributor:*
Colin Harber Stuart

With thanks to Victoria Skelton for the proofreading.

ISBN: 978 1 84762 317 1

Groovy website: www.cgpbooks.co.uk
Jolly bits of clipart from CorelDRAW®
Printed by Elanders Ltd, Newcastle upon Tyne.

Based on the classic CGP style created by Richard Parsons.

Photocopying – it's dull, grey and sometimes a bit naughty. Luckily, it's dead cheap, easy and quick to order more copies of this book from CGP – just call us on 0870 750 1242. Phew!

# Why Businesses Exist

There are a lot of businesses out there — of all different sizes, in all sorts of industries. But even the biggest and most successful firms had to start somewhere, and at one point they were all just bright ideas...

## Businesses are Set Up for Various Reasons

Businesses are organisations that provide goods or services to customers. Most businesses start when somebody decides that they can make goods or provide a service that people will be willing to pay for.

Different people start up businesses for different reasons:

1) Financial reasons — e.g. making a huge fortune from the firm's profits, or just a steady income.

2) Personal reasons — e.g. the independence of being their own boss, difficulties finding a job elsewhere, or a desire to see their ideas for a product put into practice.

3) To help others — by starting a charity, for example.

## Businesses Can Have Different Aims

Different businesses may aim to achieve different things. Most businesses have one main aim...

1) The most important aim for the vast majority of businesses is to make a profit in order to survive. If a business doesn't make a profit it's likely to go bust.

Businesses will usually have other aims too. For example...

2) Some will try to be the biggest in their market.

3) Others may try to provide the highest quality product possible.

4) Some might focus on expanding the business as much or as quickly as possible.

5) Other possible aims include satisfying customers, or trying to limit the environmental damage caused.

See page 6 for more on business aims.

D'oh... forgot to make a profit

1) Some businesses won't try to make a profit though (at least, not for their owners).

2) This is either because they are a 'not-for-profit' organisation (e.g. a charity) or they are in the public sector (which means they're owned by the government).

3) Not-for-profit organisations and public sector businesses need to earn enough income to cover their costs. Any surplus is then put back into the business.

4) Some profit-seeking businesses exist to achieve social objectives such as providing help for the homeless, or farmers in poorer countries. They're called social enterprises or 'more than profit' organisations. This is because their main aim is to use the profit that they make for the benefit of society.

## I'd stick to the public sector — or you could end up in deep profit...

Well that's an easy enough page to start with. Make sure you know why businesses exist and why people start them up. You should also know what the main aims of the different types of businesses are. Cover up the page, scribble it all down, and then check that you didn't forget anything. Champion.

2

# Enterprise

Enterprise can mean either a business or organisation, or the personal qualities that mean you can see and take advantage of new business opportunities (e.g. "That boy will go far — he's got enterprise").

## Entrepreneurs Take Advantage of Business Opportunities

1) Enterprise involves identifying new business opportunities, and then taking advantage of them. There's always a risk of failure, but the reward for a successful enterprise activity is profit.

2) Enterprise can involve starting up a new business, or helping an existing one to expand by coming up with new ideas.

3) A good business idea is usually a product/service that no other business is already providing but which customers will be willing to pay for — i.e. there's a gap in the market.

> An entrepreneur is someone who takes on the risks of enterprise activity.

4) A market niche (or niche market) is a similar idea. A market niche is a small part of the overall market, and is made up of customers with a particular need. Big companies often don't bother trying to make products for niche markets, so they're great opportunities for small companies.

## Enterprise Means Taking Risks

Enterprises always involve balancing risks against possible rewards.

1) An entrepreneur needs to gather together all the resources needed to start or expand a business. The key resource is money, which is needed to buy equipment and pay workers.

2) Very often an entrepreneur will use their own money, but they'll probably need to raise more from banks or other investors as well.

3) An entrepreneur will hope that the business will make enough profit to pay back any money that's been borrowed. If not, the business will fail and the entrepreneur will lose all the money that's been invested in the company.

4) A good entrepreneur will take a calculated risk — they'll do research, plan the business carefully to make sure it has a good chance of success, and weigh up the consequences of failure. If the risk is worth taking, the entrepreneur will go ahead with the new business venture.

## Entrepreneurs Need Particular Qualities

A successful entrepreneur is likely to have most of the following qualities:

> I can't see any of those round toffee ones. I need that particular quality Jones!

- the ability to think ahead — to identify opportunities for the future
- initiative — to seek out or seize business opportunities
- drive and determination — to turn ideas into practice
- decisiveness — so they don't shy away from making tough decisions
- networking skills — to identify people who can provide money or other resources
- leadership skills and powers of persuasion — to motivate other people to support their ideas
- a willingness to take calculated risks — and to profit from their enterprise activities
- an ability to plan carefully — to minimise the risk of failure
- an ability to learn from mistakes — and to see mistakes as "part of learning to succeed"

## Enterprise — think Dragons' Den... (or Star Trek if that's more your thing)

Bit of a funny page this one, all about concepts and personal qualities and risk taking. But funny or not, you need to make sure you know everything on this page. Yep, all of it. Even that bit right up there at the top.

# Business Ownership Structures

Every business needs to have an appropriate <u>legal structure</u>. There are a few different types to choose from — including <u>sole trader</u>, <u>partnership</u> and <u>private limited company</u>. You need to know what they are, the <u>differences</u> between them and the <u>advantages</u> and <u>disadvantages</u> of each.

## ① Sole Traders — the Easiest Business to Start

Most <u>small businesses</u> are sole traders. You don't need to do anything except <u>start trading</u>. Examples include plumbers, hairdressers, newsagents and fishmongers.

Sole Traders — Advantages

1) They're <u>dead easy</u> to set up. Get an idea and you're in business.

2) You get to be your <u>own boss</u>.

3) You alone decide what happens to any <u>profit</u>.

I'm a sole trader

Sole Traders — Disadvantages

1) You have to work <u>long hours</u>. You don't get many holidays either.

2) You have <u>unlimited liability</u>. This means that if the business goes bust owing £10 million, you may have to sell <u>everything you own</u> to pay your <u>debts</u>.

## ② Partnerships are Like Two or More Sole Traders

Partnerships are <u>not that common</u> — but you get them a lot in jobs like accountancy, solicitors and doctors.

Partners have an <u>equal say</u> in making <u>decisions</u> and an <u>equal share</u> of the <u>profits</u> — unless they have an agreement called a <u>deed of partnership</u> that says different.

Partnerships — Advantages

1) More owners means <u>more ideas</u>, and more people to <u>share the work</u>.

2) More owners means <u>more capital</u> (money) can be put into the business.

About turn!

Full steam ahead!

Partnerships — Disadvantages

1) Each partner is <u>legally responsible</u> for what all the <u>other</u> partners do.

2) Like sole traders, most partnerships have <u>unlimited liability</u>. However some partnerships can have <u>limited liability</u> — see next page for more about "limited liability".

3) More owners means more <u>disagreements</u>. You're not the only boss. If the partners disagree about <u>which direction</u> the business should go in and <u>how much</u> time to put in, it can get unpleasant.

## Wanted: Soul Trader — must have own hood and scythe...

<u>Unlimited liability</u> is really important. Examiners <u>love</u> testing you on it. Memorise the advantages and disadvantages of <u>sole traders</u> and <u>partnerships</u>, then cover up the page and write them all down. Such fun.

# Business Ownership Structures

Just one more ownership structure to go (for now, anyway — there's another one on page 43, but that's for another time). If you've ever wondered what '<u>Ltd</u>' means after a company name, then wonder no more...

## ③ Private Limited Companies — Ownership Is Restricted

<u>Limited companies</u> have some important differences to other companies.

1) They have <u>limited liability</u> so the owners only risk losing the money they invest in the business — no matter how big its debts are.

2) They must have a <u>Memorandum of Association</u>.
   This tells the world <u>who</u> the business is and <u>where</u> it is based.

3) They must also have an <u>Article of Association</u>.
   This sets out <u>how</u> the business will be run.

4) Limited liability companies are owned by <u>shareholders</u>.
   The <u>more shares</u> you own, the <u>more control</u> you get.

Hmm... there's limited company in this bar

<u>Private</u> limited companies are firms whose shares can only be sold if <u>all the shareholders</u> agree.
The shareholders are often all from the same family. Private limited companies have <u>Ltd.</u> after their name.

| Private Limited Companies — Advantages | Private Limited Companies — Disadvantages |
|---|---|
| The <u>big advantage</u> over sole traders and partnerships is <u>limited liability</u> — you can't lose more than you invest. | 1) They're <u>more expensive</u> to set up than partnerships because of all the <u>legal paperwork</u> you have to do.<br><br>2) Unlike sole traders or partnerships, the company is <u>legally obliged</u> to <u>publish its accounts</u> every year. |

## Limited Liability Companies Have Their Own Identity

The key thing about a limited liability company is that it has a <u>separate legal identity</u>.

1) Now then... <u>people</u> can do various things, such as <u>own</u> money and property, <u>make</u> contracts, <u>take</u> legal action against people (or have legal action taken against them), <u>pay</u> tax, and so on.

2) A limited liability company can <u>also</u> do <u>all</u> of these things, completely separately from its owners. So any money that the company owns is in its <u>own</u> bank account, not the owners'. If a <u>company</u> borrows money and can't pay it back, it's the <u>company</u> that's in trouble — not the owners. If it breaks the law, it's the <u>company</u> that could get fined, and so on. That's how limited liability works.

*This is basically what limited liability means. But don't think that <u>individuals</u> can <u>never</u> get into trouble — e.g. directors running the company have a legal obligation to act <u>responsibly</u>.*

3) Limited liability companies also have their own list of 'chores'.
   They have to <u>pay</u> their taxes, <u>publish</u> their accounts, and so on.

4) Limited liability companies even form <u>relationships</u> (sort of). Limited liability companies will have a range of <u>stakeholders</u> (see page 8) — and the bigger the business, the more stakeholders there are likely to be (more employees, more customers, more suppliers, and so on).

## Limited lie-ability — you can't help telling the truth...

As long as you can stand doing all the <u>paperwork</u>, there really aren't that many disadvantages to becoming a limited liability company. This '<u>separate identity</u>' thing is a <u>bit</u> like an avatar in a video game. People (the directors) get to <u>decide</u> what the company does, but they don't suffer the consequences <u>personally</u>.

# Franchises

Franchises are very popular these days, so they're a favourite topic with the examiners...

## A Franchise Is the Right to Sell Another Firm's Products

1) Some companies give other firms the right to sell their products (or use their trademarks) in return for a fee. This is known as franchising.

2) The product manufacturers are known as franchisors and the firms selling their products are franchisees.

3) Some franchises trade under the name of the franchisee but advertise that they sell a particular manufacturer's products. Car dealerships are an example of this type of franchise.

4) Branded franchises go one stage further. The franchisee buys the right to trade under the name of the franchisor, and pays them either a flat fee or a percentage of the profits. As far as the public are concerned it appears that they are buying from the franchisor, not a different firm.

5) Most of the big firms in the fast-food industry sell their products through branded-franchise outlets.

6) There are advantages to operating as a franchisee — the business model is proven to be successful and the franchisor can provide support with marketing, training and accounting. This can really help a new firm.

7) However, franchisees don't have as much control over their business as independent businesses do.

## There are Pros and Cons to Franchising

Here's a franchise case (ho ho) study...

Ryan wants to run his own café. He's considering buying a franchise in an established and extremely successful chain of cafés called Mathilda's. He's visited a few other branches of Mathilda's and knows it's always fully booked at weekends and that the food is high quality and popular. But before he signs up to anything, he weighs up the advantages and disadvantages of operating as a franchisee.

### Advantages

- He'd be buying the rights to sell an established product (e.g. high quality food, good reputation) so there's less risk of the business failing. He's also more likely to get a bank loan to help start up.
- He'd possibly benefit from wider marketing, as the franchisor may help promote the brand.
- The franchisor might provide training in how to run the café, as well as helping with things like staff management and accounting.

### Disadvantages

- He'd only be able to sell the products of the franchise so couldn't create his own menu.
- He'd have to run the café according to the franchisor's rules, so his freedom would be limited. This might mean sticking to particular furniture, decorating, opening hours, etc.

Franchisors have to consider the pros and cons of expanding their business by franchising:

**PROS:** They can increase their market share without increasing the size of their own firm — this is a very profitable way to expand (see p.41).

**CONS:** If a franchisee has poor standards (e.g. for customer service), the franchisor's brand could get a bad reputation.

## A French fries franchise — who'd have thought it...

OK then, you need to know what a franchise is, and the benefits and disadvantages of setting up business as a franchisee rather than independently. Read it, learn it, scribble it all down, live happily ever after.

# Aims, Objectives and Business Success

Businesses need to have <u>aims</u> — overall <u>goals</u> that they want to achieve.

## Success for a Business Can Mean Different Things

### SURVIVAL

Over two thirds of new businesses close within five years of starting, so just <u>surviving</u> is the main and most important <u>short-term</u> aim of all new businesses.

### PROFIT

The vast majority of businesses will aim to make a <u>profit</u>. However, this may take a few years for a new firm to achieve. Profitable firms are an important source of <u>wealth creation</u> for the <u>economy</u>.

### GROWTH

Many firms will aim to <u>grow</u>, but growth can mean different things. For example, it might mean <u>increasing the number of employees</u>, <u>increasing the number of products sold</u>, or <u>increasing income from sales</u>.

### MARKET SHARE

When a business first starts up it has zero market share... so one of its first aims is to capture a part of the market and <u>establish</u> itself. It can then aim to increase it. (This is really just another type of growth.)

Market share is found by <u>dividing</u> the <u>sales</u> of the <u>firm's products</u> by the <u>total sales</u> of the <u>market</u> (and multiplying by 100%).

Chows Chinese has a big market share already, but New Noodles might want to try and increase its share of the market.

Pepper's Pizza
Chow's Chinese
Korma's Curries
New Noodles
Fisher's Chips

### ENVIRONMENTAL SUSTAINABILITY

Environmental sustainability is about minimising the <u>impact</u> of the firm's activities on the <u>environment</u>. As consumers become more concerned about issues such as climate change, they're more likely to buy from businesses that reduce their effect (and the effect of their products) on the environment.

### ETHICAL CONSIDERATIONS

<u>Ethical considerations</u> mean thinking about whether the company acts in a way that <u>society</u> believes is <u>morally right</u> (e.g. many consumers think that it's <u>wrong</u> to test cosmetics on animals).

### CUSTOMER SATISFACTION

<u>Customer satisfaction</u> measures how <u>happy</u> consumers are with the products and services provided by the firm. The firm can <u>measure</u> this by carrying out <u>customer opinion surveys</u>, a type of <u>market research</u> (see page 14).

## Survival — also the main aim during exam time...

So, just <u>seven types</u> of <u>business aims</u> to learn here — couldn't be easier. Well OK, it would be easier if there were, say, four types of business aims. Or three. Or (in an ideal world) just the one. But seven's not bad. And once you've got your head round <u>aims</u> we can head off into the exciting world of <u>objectives</u>. Oooh...

# Aims, Objectives and Business Success

Objectives are a bit like aims, but they're usually more short-term. They're a bit like stepping stones on the way to an aim, if you like. Yeah... think of it like that... I like that mental picture.

## Objectives Help Businesses Achieve Their Aims

1) Once a firm has established its aims, it needs to set business objectives.

2) Just like with aims, there are different types of objectives. They can be related to survival, profit, growth, market share, customer satisfaction or ethical and environmental issues.

3) Objectives are more specific than aims — they're measurable steps on the way to the aim. So, if a firm's aim is to grow, an objective might be to increase income from sales by 30% over two years.

4) Or, if the aim was to improve the firm's environmental sustainability, an objective might be to increase usage of recycled materials in the production process from 20% to 50% within the next six months.

5) Once objectives have been set they act as clear targets for firms to work towards.

6) They can then be used later to measure whether a firm has been successful or not.

## Businesses Use their Objectives to Measure Success

Companies compare their actual performance to the objectives they've set.
They do this in different ways, depending on the nature of the objectives.

### FOR OBJECTIVES WITH NUMERICAL TARGETS, COMPARE THESE TARGETS AGAINST ACTUAL PERFORMANCE

For example, a business could set itself targets of...

- £10,000 sales, and profits of £1000, after one year

- increasing sales by 5% and profits by 10% every year after this for the next five years.

At the end of each year, the business can measure how well it has met these targets, and take action to improve its performance. If it found the first target was easy to meet, it might decide to make the later targets harder — for example, increase profits by 15% each year.

Our profits really started taking off in 2003...

### NON-NUMERICAL TARGETS CAN BE TRICKIER TO USE

It's simple to set targets for things that can be described as a number (e.g. sales and profits). It's more difficult for "soft" aims such as "behaving in an ethical way". There are a couple of alternatives...

- A business could list some ethical activities it will do, and some unethical activities which it won't do — then it can check later whether it has kept its promises.

- Or a business can conduct impact assessments — these are surveys (sometimes done by researchers with no connection to the business) to find out what stakeholders think of the business's behaviour. For example it could carry out an environmental impact assessment.

## Objectively, I think this page has been a success...

Maybe objectives weren't quite as exciting as I made out... But they are pretty good... Well, I think they are. Anyway, exciting or not, you need to know what objectives are, why they're useful and how they can be used to measure success. OK, I admit it, they're not exciting at all. But they are important. So learn 'em.

# The Influence of Stakeholders

A <u>stakeholder</u> is <u>anyone</u> who's affected by a business. So even small businesses may have lots of stakeholders.

## There are Different Types of Stakeholders

1) Stakeholders may be <u>internal</u> or <u>external</u>.

2) <u>Internal</u> stakeholders are <u>inside</u> the firm. They include the <u>owners</u> (or the <u>shareholders</u> in a limited company) and the <u>employees</u>.

3) <u>External</u> stakeholders are <u>outside</u> the firm. They include <u>customers</u>, <u>suppliers</u>, the <u>local community</u> and the <u>government</u>.

*I thought you said steakholder.*

## Different Stakeholders Have Different Ideas of Success

Different stakeholders are affected by the business in different ways. This means they have different <u>opinions</u> about what makes a firm <u>successful</u> and what its <u>objectives</u> should be. For example:

**1** <u>Employees</u> are interested in their <u>job security</u> and <u>promotion prospects</u>. These are improved if the firm is <u>profitable</u> and <u>growing</u>. Employees also want a <u>decent wage</u> and <u>good working conditions</u>. So they may benefit most when objectives are based on <u>profitability</u>, <u>growth</u> and <u>ethics</u>.

**2** <u>Suppliers</u> are who the firm <u>buys raw materials</u> from. The firm provides them with their income. If the firm is profitable and grows they'll need more materials and the supplier will get more business. So suppliers benefit most when the firm sets objectives based on <u>profitability</u> and <u>growth</u>.

**3** The <u>local community</u> where the business is based will suffer if the firm causes <u>noise and pollution</u>. They may gain if the firm provides <u>good jobs</u> and <u>sponsors</u> local activities. So the local community may benefit when objectives are based on <u>environmental sustainability</u>, <u>ethical considerations</u>, <u>profitability</u> and <u>growth</u>.

**4** <u>Customers</u> want <u>high quality</u> products at <u>low prices</u>. They benefit when objectives are based on <u>customer satisfaction</u>.

**5** The <u>government</u> will receive <u>taxes</u> if the firm makes a <u>profit</u>. They may benefit most when objectives are based on <u>profitability</u>, <u>growth</u>, or <u>job creation</u>.

## Stakeholders Influence Objectives to Varying Degrees

The <u>owners</u> are the most important stakeholders. They decide what happens to the business. However...

1) No business can ignore its <u>customers</u>. If it can't sell its products it won't survive.

2) And if a business doesn't have happy workers it may become <u>unproductive</u>.

3) But a company may not mind being <u>unpopular</u> in the <u>local community</u> if it sells most of its products somewhere else.

*I thought you said stay colder.*

4) So, the owners need to consider the interests of <u>other stakeholders</u> when they're setting their objectives. They may decide to <u>ignore</u> the needs of some but they'll need to take others into account if they want to <u>survive</u> as a firm.

## Stakeholders — vampires are terrified of them...

This is <u>really simple</u>. People affected by a business are called stakeholders and they can <u>influence</u> a firm's <u>objectives</u>. Just remember it's <u>stake</u>holder, not <u>steak</u>holder. Unless you want to look like a proper muppet.

# The Business Plan

It's vital that the business has a <u>clear idea</u> of what it's going to do if it wants to be successful — this is where the <u>business plan</u> comes in.  You need to know <u>why</u> businesses have them and <u>what</u> they should contain.

## The Plan is for the Owner and Financial Backers

1) A <u>business plan</u> is an outline of <u>what</u> a new business will do, and <u>how</u> it aims to do it.

2) Creating a business plan forces the owner to <u>think carefully</u> about what the business is going to do and what <u>resources</u> are needed.  This will allow them to calculate how much <u>start-up capital</u> is needed.

3) The plan can be used to <u>convince financial backers</u> (e.g. banks) that the business is a <u>sound investment</u>.

4) If the business is a <u>bad idea</u>, the <u>planning</u> should help the owner or the financial backers realise this at an <u>early stage</u> — before they've wasted <u>time and money</u> on a business that was never going to work.

## Most Plans Include At Least Seven Sections

There is no single <u>correct way</u> to write a business plan — but most good 'uns include all of the stuff below.
There's also usually an <u>executive summary</u> at the start to summarise the whole thing.

1. `PERSONAL DETAILS` of the <u>owner</u> and other <u>important personnel</u> — like their <u>CVs</u>.
   Financial backers will want to know who they are trusting with their money.

2. `MISSION STATEMENT` — a way of describing the <u>broad aims</u> of the company.
   They usually use long words to say something <u>general and obvious</u>, e.g. "To combine fresh bread and tasty fillings in popular combinations and become the market leading sandwich shop in Kent."

3. `OBJECTIVES` are more <u>specific</u> than aims, e.g. "To average 160 sandwich sales per lunchtime over 4 years."

4. `PRODUCT DESCRIPTION` — including details of the <u>market</u> and <u>competitors</u>.  It should explain how the firm will achieve <u>product differentiation</u> — also called its <u>unique selling point (USP)</u>.
   It should also describe its <u>marketing strategy</u> using the <u>4 Ps</u> (p.12).
   All statements should be supported by <u>field or desk research</u> (p.14).

> Mission statement: by a studied combination of irresistible charm and feigned nonchalance, to strive to attain greater levels of social and physical intimacy with Cathy Bloggs of 11B.

5. `PRODUCTION DETAILS` — how the firm will make its product or provide its service.  It should list all the <u>equipment</u> needed and its <u>location</u>.

6. `STAFFING REQUIREMENTS` What <u>personnel</u> will be needed — <u>how many</u> people, their <u>job descriptions</u> and the expected <u>wage bill</u>.

7. `FINANCE` It should explain how much <u>money</u> is needed to <u>start up</u> the business.  There should be a <u>cash flow</u> forecast and a projected <u>profit and loss account</u> and <u>balance sheet</u>.  There should also be <u>ratios</u> to show any backer the <u>likely return</u> on their investment.

> All these financial bits and bobs are covered in Section 8 — (they're for AQA Unit 2).

## A Good Business Plan is No Guarantee of Success

Starting a business involves many <u>risks</u> and <u>uncertainties</u>, some of which can't be controlled.  These include:

1) the health of the <u>economy</u>.  The UK entered a sharp recession in 2009 that very few people predicted.  Many businesses closed as a result.

2) the <u>actions of competitors</u>.  Few businesses know what its competitors are planning — especially if new firms are planning to enter the market with innovative ideas.  A successful business constantly <u>monitors</u> its plan and the factors which affect success — e.g. by regularly carrying out <u>market</u> and <u>competitor research</u>.

## Fear not Mr. Bank Manager — for I have a cunning plan...

The best laid business plans <u>might not stop</u> a fledgling business from <u>going under</u> — but anyone starting a firm <u>without one</u> would need improbable amounts of luck to survive.  In short, plans are <u>important</u>.  Learn.

# Location of Production

All firms, whether they produce goods or provide services, have to decide <u>where to locate</u>. It's usually a compromise between producing where it's <u>cheapest</u> and being where they would generate the <u>most income</u>. There are <u>other factors</u> which are also important — depending on the industry.

## Location is Influenced by Nine Main Factors

Suppose a new startup company Granite King are looking for a location for their new kitchen worktops manufacturing business. They'll want to think about these things...

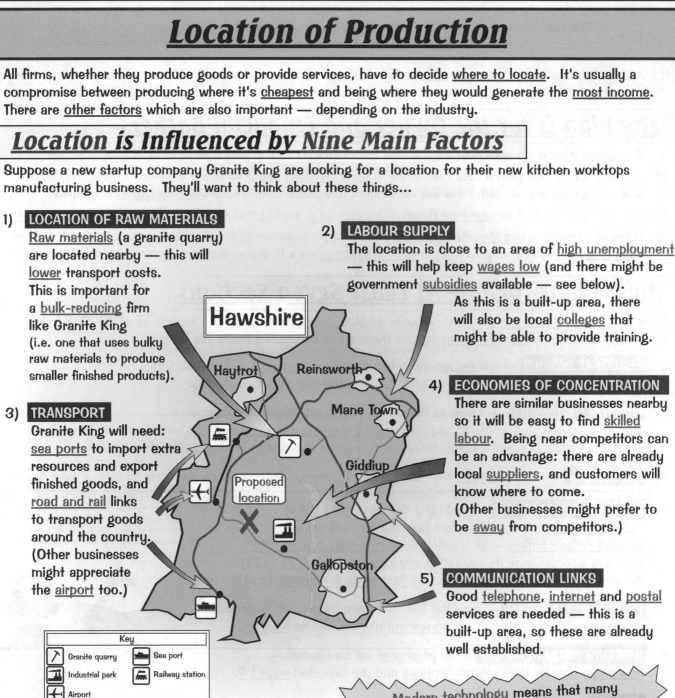

**1) LOCATION OF RAW MATERIALS**
<u>Raw materials</u> (a granite quarry) are located nearby — this will <u>lower</u> transport costs. This is important for a <u>bulk-reducing</u> firm like Granite King (i.e. one that uses bulky raw materials to produce smaller finished products).

**2) LABOUR SUPPLY**
The location is close to an area of <u>high unemployment</u> — this will help keep <u>wages low</u> (and there might be government <u>subsidies</u> available — see below). As this is a built-up area, there will also be local <u>colleges</u> that might be able to provide training.

**3) TRANSPORT**
Granite King will need: <u>sea ports</u> to import extra resources and export finished goods, and <u>road and rail</u> links to transport goods around the country. (Other businesses might appreciate the <u>airport</u> too.)

**4) ECONOMIES OF CONCENTRATION**
There are similar businesses nearby so it will be easy to find <u>skilled labour</u>. Being near competitors can be an advantage: there are already local <u>suppliers</u>, and customers will know where to come. (Other businesses might prefer to be <u>away</u> from competitors.)

**5) COMMUNICATION LINKS**
Good <u>telephone</u>, <u>internet</u> and <u>postal</u> services are needed — this is a built-up area, so these are already well established.

> <u>Modern technology</u> means that many businesses can trade over the <u>internet</u>. This means they can be more <u>flexible</u> about their location — they can maybe even locate abroad.

Hawshire

Haytrot
Reinsworth
Mane Town
Giddiup
Proposed location
Gallopston

**Key**
↗ Granite quarry    ⛴ Sea port
🏭 Industrial park    🚂 Railway station
✈ Airport

Other businesses might consider these factors:

**6) LOCATION OF THE MARKET** Firms like breweries pay more to transport their finished products than their raw materials. These <u>bulk-increasing firms</u> find it cheapest to locate near to their <u>customers</u>. Some <u>services</u>, such as dentists and florists, locate where people can easily get to them.

**7) GOVERNMENT POLICY** Governments often pay <u>big multinationals</u> to locate in their country. Or they may give subsidies or tax breaks to firms locating in areas of <u>high unemployment</u>.

## Location of the market — it's on the High Street, mate...

Each of these factors will be important in <u>some</u> industries but <u>not</u> in others.
Think of a few <u>industries</u> — decide what location location location factors would be important for them.

# Revision Summary for Section One

Okay, so that's the first section over with — now it's time to find out how much you remember. Have a bash at these questions. If you can do them all, pat yourself on the back and feel smug. If you can't, then go back and look at the section again and keep plugging away until you can answer them all. Yes, I know it's a pain but life's like that — and after all, it's the only way you're going to get ready for the exam.

1) Give two reasons why someone might start a business.

2) Do charities aim to make a profit?

3) What is a social enterprise?

4) What is meant by a calculated risk?

5) List five qualities that an entrepreneur is likely to have.

6) Which two of these are problems if you're a sole trader?
                     a) long hours;   b) unlimited liability;   c) smelly fish.

7) What does a sole trader gain and lose if it becomes a partnership?

8) If you own part of a business and the business goes bankrupt, would you rather have limited or unlimited liability? Why?

9) 'Limited companies have a separate legal identity.' What does this mean?

10) What is a franchise?

11) Describe two benefits of franchising for the franchisee.

12) Describe two disadvantages of franchising for the franchisee.

13) List seven types of business aim.

14) Explain the difference between a business aim and a business objective.

15) Describe one use of business objectives.

16) Describe how a business could use numerical targets to assess its performance over a year.

17) Describe how a business could determine whether it's met its objectives for 'being ethical'.

18) What is a stakeholder?

19) Name two internal stakeholders.

20) Name two external stakeholders.

21) Explain why the shareholders of a business and consumers might have different opinions about how successful the business is.

22) Who are the most important stakeholders and why?

23) Describe the purpose of a business plan.

24) Describe the things that should be included in a business plan.

25) Why isn't a good business plan a guarantee of success?

26) Why might some firms choose to locate production closer to their raw materials than their customers?

27) List four other factors that need to be considered when choosing a business location.

# The Marketing Mix

Human beings have <u>needs</u> — essential things like water, food and shelter. Once our needs are satisfied, we start to <u>want</u> luxuries, and we're prepared to <u>pay</u> for them. <u>Marketing</u> is about coming up with a <u>product</u> that people need or want — then making it as <u>easy as possible</u> for them to buy it. Sounds simple enough...

## There are Four Ps in Marketing

There are four <u>elements</u> to marketing, <u>product</u>, <u>price</u>, <u>promotion</u> and <u>place</u> — the four Ps. They're the <u>key</u> to understanding what marketing is all about. If a firm gets them <u>right</u> it will be <u>easy</u> to sell its product. If it gets <u>even one</u> of them <u>wrong</u>, it's in <u>trouble</u>.

Together the four Ps are called the MARKETING MIX .

But I can't see any Ps in marketing...

### 1) PRODUCT

The firm must come up with a <u>product</u> that people will <u>want to buy</u>. It must <u>fulfil</u> some of the customer's <u>needs or wants</u> if it's going to sell. So spinach flavoured sweets, for example, probably wouldn't sell that well.

Spinach sweets! Finally here to fulfill my every want and need!

### 2) PRICE

The <u>price</u> must be one that the customer thinks is good <u>value for money</u>. This isn't the same as being cheap. You might be prepared to pay a <u>lot of money</u> for a brand new, 50-inch plasma-screen TV, but you'd expect an old basic 12-inch model to be much <u>cheaper</u>.

### 3) PROMOTION

The product must be <u>promoted</u> so that potential customers are <u>aware</u> that it exists. It doesn't matter how <u>good</u> the product is, — if no-one knows about it no-one will buy it.

### 4) PLACE

It must be sold in a <u>place</u> that the customer will find <u>convenient</u>. That's why you can buy buckets and spades at the beach, goggles at the swimming baths, and petrol at roadside service stations — they're the <u>most convenient places</u> for people to buy these products.

## The Marketing Mix is Different for Different Products

1) Depending on the situation, some of the Ps might be <u>more important</u> than others.

2) For example, if customers <u>really want</u> the <u>product</u>, or it's in a <u>really convenient place</u>, they may be prepared to pay a <u>higher price</u>.

3) Alternatively, customers may be prepared to go to a <u>less convenient place</u>, or buy a product that isn't <u>exactly</u> what they <u>want</u> if the <u>price is lower</u>.

4) Customers' needs and wants usually <u>change</u> over time — a business should <u>adapt</u> its marketing mix to <u>meet</u> these changing needs.

5) For example, customers used to buy music on <u>vinyl records</u> from a <u>shop</u>. Nowadays they're more likely to <u>download</u> music from the <u>internet</u>. The <u>product</u> and <u>place</u> have changed.

Well, it's not the luxury model I had in mind, but it certainly is cheap...

## I want it all — and I want it now (in the right place at the right price, please)...

Customers are <u>absolutely crucial</u> to marketing. A good marketing mix makes customers want to <u>spend money</u> on your product. But customers' needs <u>change</u> — so the marketing mix also needs to change to keep up.

# More About Marketing

For businesses to succeed they need to understand <u>their place</u> in the market and have good ideas for <u>products</u> — they have to know who their customers <u>are</u>, what they <u>need</u>, and whether these needs are being <u>met</u>.

## Businesses Have to Decide on a Marketing Strategy

1) Businesses develop <u>marketing strategies</u> to maximise their <u>sales</u> and make the best use of their <u>resources</u>. Before deciding on a strategy, businesses need to analyse <u>themselves</u> and <u>other factors</u> in the market.

2) Analysing their <u>strengths</u> and <u>weaknesses</u> can give firms ideas for new products and how to market them. For example, a common weakness of small businesses is a <u>lack of funding</u>. This means there probably won't be a lot of money available for promotion — the marketing strategy needs to take this into account.

3) It's really important for new businesses to analyse the <u>market</u> as well — it can help them to come up with ideas for new <u>products</u> and identify <u>gaps in the market</u> (see below). One way that businesses can do this is by <u>mapping the market</u>.

## Businesses Map the Market to Find Information

<u>Mapping the market</u> helps a business understand its <u>location</u> within the market, and the market's <u>key features</u>. The kinds of information shown in a market map might include...

1) How many <u>customers</u> are in the market and how much they <u>spend</u>.
2) Which <u>segments</u> the customers belong to. (Segments are <u>categories</u> of people — they're usually based on <u>age</u>, <u>social class</u>, <u>gender</u>, <u>location</u>, <u>culture</u> or <u>religion</u>.)
3) Which products are <u>popular</u> and <u>unpopular</u>.
4) <u>Competitors</u> selling similar products and <u>where</u> they sell them.

**Market Map for Instant Coffee**

Premium Price / Budget Price / Low Quality / High Quality
Mountain Grind, Get Me Up, Full-o-Beans, Supercharge, Bonka Café, Café Toujours, Brown and Dirty, Roast Away

**THE MARKET**
Customer (needy) / Customers / Unpopular Product / Dragons' den / Here be competitors / Popular Product / Treasure / YOU ARE HERE

*Note: this diagram isn't a serious example. Thank you.*

Market maps are often in the form of a <u>diagram</u>, but there are different kinds. Here's a couple of examples...

## Gaps in the Market Provide Opportunities for Firms

1) Sometimes a group of customers will have a need that <u>isn't being met</u>. This is known as a <u>gap in the market</u>.

2) A business needs to move quickly to fill the gap — <u>before</u> its competitors do. It needs to develop a way to meet the customers' needs.

3) This might mean developing a new <u>product</u>. For example, a firm selling fruit smoothies could spot a gap in the market for vegetable smoothies, or for a new fruit smoothie flavour.

4) Or it might mean selling an existing product in a new <u>place</u> or at a new <u>price</u>, or maybe just <u>promoting</u> it in a new way to convince customers it's just what they need.

5) A gap in the market can be a great <u>opportunity</u> for a small business. If it gets the marketing mix right, a gap can <u>expand</u> into a large market.

## My weakness is none of your business...

Actually, that was just the name of a pop song (ask your Dad). In the real world, if firms want to succeed they need to know their <u>strengths</u> and <u>weaknesses</u>, and then jump on any <u>opportunity</u> that floats along.

# Market Research

Marketing is all about giving <u>customers</u> what they <u>want</u>. Sounds simple enough — as long as you <u>know</u> what the customers want. And to find that out you need to enter the wonderful world of <u>market research</u>...

## Market Research Finds Out What Customers Want

1) A business would be in real trouble if it spent time and money producing and promoting a product that no-one wanted to <u>buy</u>, so market research is really <u>important</u>.

2) It's used to find out what <u>products</u> consumers want, what <u>price</u> they're willing to pay for them and their current <u>buying habits</u>. It can also be used to gather information on the products and prices of <u>competitors</u>.

3) The problem with market research is that it costs <u>money</u> and most new businesses have a <u>limited budget</u>.

4) So firms need to think carefully about the <u>best way</u> to carry out their research. They need to find out what customers want without spending <u>too much money</u>.

5) There are <u>two main types</u> of market research — <u>field research</u> and <u>desk research</u>.

## Field Research is Doing Your Own Donkey Work

1) Field research is also called <u>primary</u> research or <u>original</u> research. It involves things like <u>questionnaires</u>, <u>telephone surveys</u>, <u>customer/supplier feedback</u> and <u>focus groups</u>.

2) It's useful for finding out <u>new information</u>, and getting <u>customers' views</u> on your products.

3) A business can't ask <u>every</u> potential customer for their views — they generally just ask a <u>sample</u> of people.

4) <u>Large samples</u> are the most <u>accurate</u> but also the most <u>expensive</u>. Small businesses may have to compromise here and use <u>small sample groups</u> to keep their costs down.

Uh-huh. And would you prefer to be ploughed up or left fallow?

5) Firms can also save on costs by carrying out research over the <u>telephone</u> or <u>internet</u> rather than in person — this is especially useful for small firms.

6) They may also use <u>focus groups</u> — where a small group of people are asked to <u>discuss</u> their attitudes towards a product.

7) Field research provides data that's <u>up to date</u>, <u>relevant</u> and <u>specific</u> to your products. But on the downside, it's <u>expensive</u>, and can be <u>time-consuming</u>.

## Desk Research is Looking at Other People's Work

1) Desk research is also called <u>secondary</u> research or <u>published</u> research.

2) Desk research gives businesses access to a <u>wide range</u> of data — not just the views of their sample groups. It's useful for looking at the <u>whole market</u>, and analysing <u>past trends</u> to predict the future.

3) It involves looking at things like <u>market research reports</u> (such as Mintel), <u>government publications</u> (such as the Family Expenditure Survey or Social Trends), and articles in <u>newspapers</u>, <u>magazines</u> and on the <u>internet</u>.

4) It's often used by small businesses as it's <u>cheaper</u> than field research, and the data is <u>easily found</u> and <u>instantly available</u>.

5) Disadvantages of desk research are that it's <u>not always relevant</u> to your needs, it's <u>not specifically</u> about your products, and it's often <u>out of date</u>.

Desk News
67% of desks "are now mahogany shocker"

## Telephone surveys — don't get hung up about them...

Market research is <u>crucial</u> for <u>new businesses</u> — they need to decide what they want to <u>find out</u> about the market and then choose the <u>best method</u> for collecting the data. Or things could <u>go wrong</u> pretty quickly.

# *Products*

Once the market research is done, businesses can move onto the first of the four Ps — the <u>product</u>.

## *Products Should Be Market-Driven*

1) Some businesses use <u>market research</u> to find out <u>what people want</u>, then make it. This usually means the product is <u>useful</u> — like an MP3 player with a built-in radio. These firms are said to be <u>market-driven</u>.

2) Other firms are <u>product-driven</u> — they design or invent a <u>new product</u> and then <u>try to sell it</u>. This often means they make something nobody really wants — like an MP3 player with a built-in toaster. This can be disastrous for a business just starting out.

3) With very few exceptions, <u>market-driven</u> firms do best.

## *Smaller Firms Often Target Smaller Markets*

Many businesses are started by <u>entrepreneurs</u> who've spotted an opportunity to launch a new product whilst working for another company. This means they already have <u>ideas</u> for products and often have <u>expertise</u> in the area — really useful when starting a business. But ideas alone aren't enough — new firms need to consider their <u>target market</u> and the <u>resources available</u> to them before making a final decision on a product.

### Things to consider...

1) <u>Large established companies</u> usually cater to mass market tastes. This often leaves <u>market gaps</u> free for <u>smaller</u> firms to target. These are smaller groups of customers that large businesses may not be interested in so are good targets for small firms with <u>limited resources</u>.

2) Starting a business costs a lot of <u>money</u> and, to begin with at least, there'll be no money <u>coming in</u> from sales. New firms need to take this into account when they're deciding what <u>products</u> they're going to offer. For example...

- The cost of <u>research and development</u> (<u>R&D</u>) and <u>market research</u> — both used to develop ideas and turn them into marketable products — need to be kept to a <u>minimum</u>.
  - And products that need lots of expensive equipment to make aren't realistic options for a lot of new businesses either.

It may seem like having a small business is all doom and gloom — not much money for <u>production</u> and a limited budget for <u>market research</u> and <u>advertising</u>. But don't despair, there are <u>benefits</u> to having a small firm...

1) Small businesses find it much easier to <u>alter their products</u> to meet <u>customers' needs</u> than large firms do.

2) This is because large firms tend to have huge <u>mechanised production processes</u> involving many <u>stages</u>. They can't just interrupt or change production if a customer wants something a little bit different to what's on offer — it would cost them <u>too much money</u>.

3) Smaller firms work on a <u>smaller scale</u> — they make fewer products, using fewer people and less equipment. This means that altering the production process is <u>less disruptive</u> and <u>costs less money</u>. So it's easier for small firms to make alterations to their products. It could even allow them to make <u>bespoke products</u> (products made to the customer's own specification).

4) This leads to happy customers, who are likely to return, helping the business to <u>grow</u>. Yay. ☺

## *Time for a bit of R&D — revision and despair...*

So, small businesses can offer <u>all kinds of products</u> as long as they can <u>afford</u> to make them. And they can also <u>alter</u> them to meet their customers' <u>needs</u>. Good news. With that in mind, I'm off to find one that will adapt my MP3 player to be a toaster as well. I don't care what anyone says, I think it's a brilliant idea.

# Price — Demand and Supply

Customers like to buy things at bargain prices. Businesses like to sell things at high prices and make profits. The laws of supply and demand force them to settle their differences. I do like a happy ending.

## Demand Rises as Price Falls

1) Demand means the quantity of a product that consumers are willing and able to buy. The law of demand is that as the price increases the quantity demanded will fall.

2) The same is true the other way round — a decrease in price increases demand. There are two reasons for this. At a lower price more people can afford the product. And it becomes cheaper compared to its substitutes — that is, similar goods that people might buy instead.

3) Falls in demand and decreases in prices can both badly affect the profits of small businesses.

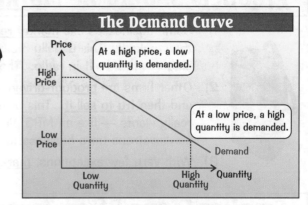

## Supply Rises as Price Rises

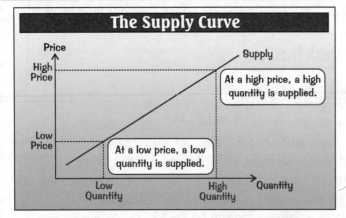

1) Supply is the quantity of a product producers are willing and able to make for sale. The law of supply is that as the price increases, the quantity supplied increases — and vice versa.

2) When the price is low, very few producers will be able to make a profit — so the supply is small. At high prices even inefficient producers can make a profit — so the supply is large.

## Equilibrium — where Producers and Consumers Agree

1) Producers want to sell at a high price and make a large profit. Consumers want to buy at a low price. The marketplace forces a clever compromise.

2) If the price is too low there'll be a shortage of supply. Some consumers will be willing to pay more, so producers increase prices.

3) If the price is too high, there'll be a surplus of supply. Producers will have to reduce prices to persuade people to buy unsold goods.

4) Eventually producers and consumers agree on the price and quantity to be exchanged. The point where they agree is called equilibrium.

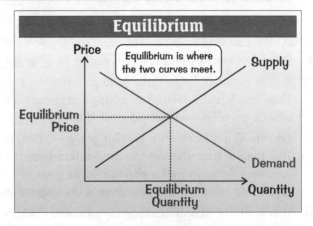

## Producers get high (prices) on their own supply...

At low prices, demand is high but supply is low. At high prices, demand is low but supply is high. Equilibrium balances things out. Easy as anything. Well, maybe not anything — but not too bad.

# Promotion and Place

How a product is promoted and where it's sold are really important parts of the marketing strategy.

## Firms Promote Their Products By Advertising

Chipper's Chip Shop
Much better than that other chip shop just down there — they're rubbish.

Advertising is any message about itself or its products that a firm has paid for. Small businesses need to advertise their products to make consumers aware of them and to persuade them to switch from rival products. The ultimate aim, of course, is to sell products so the business is successful and can grow.

## Products Can Be Advertised In Different Media

Small businesses need to use promotion methods that are suitable for their budget — which is usually fairly limited. There are loads of places firms can advertise without completely blowing the budget, For example...

1) LOCAL RADIO is a good option for small businesses. It's cheaper than TV and can be used to target small regions and listeners of particular programmes.

2) LOCAL NEWSPAPERS know a lot about their readership so it's easy to target effectively.

3) MAGAZINES are a good way for small businesses to target specialist markets over a wide area.

4) POSTERS and BILLBOARDS have a high visual impact, stay in place for a long time and can be seen daily by lots of people.

5) LEAFLETS, BUSINESS CARDS and JUNK MAIL are cheap to produce and distribute. They can be targeted at certain groups, e.g. handing out leaflets for a new clothes shop to people shopping on the high street.

## Where Firms Advertise Depends on Various Things

Where the firm will place its advertising depends on...

Dude — these doilies are sick. To the max.

1) The target audience. If you want to sell lace doilies to women over 55, don't place your advert in 'Which Skateboard' magazine.

2) The size and location of the market. If you are launching 'Death Cola' in the South West only, don't advertise in the 'North Eastern Herald'.

3) The size of the budget. Personal recommendations and handing out leaflets and business cards can be the most cost-effective advertising for cash-strapped firms.

## Place — Where the Product Will Be Sold

1) Firms need to make sure that their products are sold in a place that's convenient for potential customers.

2) The traditional route is to sell via retailers (shops). Products need to be sold in the most suitable shops — i.e. places where they'll be easily available to the target market.

3) But it's now becoming more common for manufacturers to sell direct to consumers (e.g. via factory shops, mail order and internet selling).

4) Internet sites allow even small firms (with small budgets) to reach large numbers of consumers over wide areas. Buying and selling online is called e-commerce, and in recent years it's become more and more important. E-commerce allows small businesses to promote and sell their products nationwide, and gives them access to international markets much more easily (see p37).

## My personal recommendation — learn this page.

And that advice is free. Which isn't a word you hear a lot in business. Pretty much everything has to be paid for and that's not good news for small businesses. They're left trying to squeeze lots of advertising out of a small budget, so need to know which are the most cost-effective ways to do it. And so do you.

# Revision Summary for Section Two

Well, we've run out of facts about marketing so you know what that means — time to make sure you've learned the ones I've told you about. One of them is a 'numbers' question — the answer's at the bottom of the page (so you can cheat if you want to, but it won't do you any good because you won't learn a thing that way).

You also won't learn anything if you quietly skip over these questions without actually trying to answer them. Or if you answer them and get them wrong, but assume that you'll get them right on the day without doing any extra learning. If you try any of these tactics, you're nowt but a fool to yourself. There... that's you told.

1) What are the 4 Ps in the marketing mix?

2) Why might a customer be prepared to pay a higher price than usual for a product?

3) Why are market maps useful?

4) What is a gap in the market?

5) Why is market research important?

6) Give three examples of information that market research is used to find.

7) Give two examples of field research methods.

8) Give an advantage and a disadvantage of field research.

9) Give an advantage and a disadvantage of desk research.

10) What is a market-driven firm?

11) Explain why small firms often find it easier to alter their products than large firms.

12) What is a bespoke product?

13) Why does the demand curve slope downwards?

14) Why does the supply curve slope upwards?

15) Sketch a demand and supply diagram using the data on the right.
   a) What is the equilibrium price and quantity?
   b) Which of the following is happening at a price of £6?
      i) consumers are desperate to buy and there's a shortage.
      ii) producers are making too much and there's a surplus.
   c) How about at a price of £21?

| Price (£) | Demand (thousands) | Supply (thousands) |
|---|---|---|
| 3 | 18 | 2 |
| 6 | 16 | 4 |
| 9 | 14 | 6 |
| 12 | 12 | 8 |
| 15 | 10 | 10 |
| 18 | 8 | 12 |
| 21 | 6 | 14 |
| 24 | 4 | 16 |
| 27 | 2 | 18 |

16) List four places suitable for small businesses to promote their products.

17) Describe three things that influence where a firm will advertise.

18) What is e-commerce?

19) Give an advantage of e-commerce.

20) Would you like to stop answering questions on marketing?

# Business Costs

The stuff on this page is really important — it all hinges on one simple sum: profit = revenue – cost.

## Revenue is the Income Earned by a Business

1) Businesses earn most of their income from selling their product to customers.

2) Revenue can be calculated by multiplying sales (the number of units sold) by the price (the amount the customer pays). If Britney's Spheres Ltd. sell 20,000 tennis balls at £2 each — their sales revenue will be £40,000.

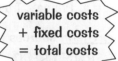

sales × price = revenue

## Costs are the Expenses Paid Out to Run the Business

### Costs can be Direct or Indirect...

1) Direct costs are expenses that can be attributed to making a particular product. Examples include costs of factory labour, raw materials and operating machinery.

2) Indirect costs are the general overheads of running the business. Examples include management salaries, telephone bills and office rent.

direct costs + indirect costs = total costs

### ...and Fixed or Variable

1) Fixed costs do not vary with output. They're mostly indirect costs. They have to be paid even if the firm produces nothing.

2) Variable costs are costs that will increase as the firm expands output. They're mostly direct costs — factory labour, raw materials and machinery.

3) Some costs are semi-variable — they only vary a little because they have a large fixed element. For example, most workers receive a basic salary and only part of their pay is linked to output.

4) Fixed costs are only fixed over a short period of time — an expanding firm's fixed costs will increase.

variable costs + fixed costs = total costs

### Average Cost is How Much Each Product Cost to Make

1) To find the average cost of making a product, divide the total cost by output (number of products made). To make a profit the firm must charge a higher price than this.

Britney's Spheres Ltd. has an output of 20,000 tennis balls, at a total cost of £30,000.
The average cost = £30,000 ÷ 20,000 = £1.50 per ball.
The selling price should be more than £1.50 per ball.

total cost ÷ output = average cost

2) Average costs usually fall as the firm gets bigger, because of economies of scale (see p71).

## Profit = Revenue – Costs

Profit (or loss) is the difference between revenue and costs over a period of time.

Britney's Spheres Ltd. sells 20,000 tennis balls in a month at £2 each.
Over the same month its total costs are £30,000.
Profit = (20,000 × £2) – £30,000 = £40,000 – £30,000 = £10,000
So the business makes £10,000 profit in the month.

Sounds like a load of balls to me.

If costs are higher than revenue, the business will make a loss instead of a profit, and the answer to the calculation above will be negative.

## Average cost — it's neither good nor bad...

Make sure you know the difference between price and cost — price is the amount paid by a customer, cost is the amount paid by the producer. Cover the page and check you can describe each type of cost. Then all you've got to do is learn what profit is and how to work it out and you'll be quids in. Groan.

# Sources of Finance

You need to know <u>why</u> firms need to <u>raise finance</u>, how they can do it and what <u>each method</u> is best used for.

## Firms Need Finance for Various Reasons

1) New firms need <u>start-up capital</u> to buy the <u>assets</u> needed to run the business.

2) New firms <u>also need</u> to finance their poor initial <u>cash flow</u> — they'll need to pay their <u>suppliers</u> before they receive money from their <u>customers</u>.

3) All firms need enough cash to meet the <u>day-to-day running</u> of the business — that's called <u>working capital</u>.

4) Sometimes customers <u>delay payment</u> — finance is needed to cover this shortfall in <u>liquidity</u> (see page 22).

5) Firms may need finance to fund <u>expansion</u> — they may be moving to larger premises.

> <u>Assets</u> are valuable items <u>owned</u> by the business (e.g. equipment, buildings).

## Small Firms Have Five Main Sources of Start-up Finance

Small firms may be <u>given</u> money in the form of <u>grants</u>, or they may be able to <u>borrow</u> it — either over a short period or a longer period.

1) GRANTS are often given to <u>qualifying</u> new or small firms e.g. businesses in areas of <u>high unemployment</u>. Grant providers include the <u>EU</u>, <u>local and national government</u> and <u>charities</u>, e.g. Prince's Trust. Unlike loans, they <u>don't</u> have to be repaid.

<u>Short-term</u> sources need to be repaid after a relatively short period of time, e.g. <u>weeks</u> or <u>months</u>.

2) TRADE CREDIT — rather than expecting the customer to pay cash on delivery, most businesses will issue them with an <u>invoice</u> — this usually gives the customer one or two months to pay. This is useful for a small firm as they have up to 60 days to <u>earn</u> the money needed to pay the debt.

3) OVERDRAFTS let the firm take <u>more money</u> out of the bank than it has in its account. <u>Interest charges</u> are high — but only while you're overdrawn.

<u>Long-term</u> sources are repaid over longer periods, usually <u>years</u>.

4) LOANS — there are <u>three types</u> of loans a small business might take out:

- <u>Bank loans</u> are quick and easy to take out — but will need to be repaid with <u>interest</u>. The bank may require <u>collateral</u> — assets the bank can <u>repossess</u> if the loan is <u>not repaid</u>.

- Loans from <u>friends and family</u>. It can be hard to <u>persuade</u> a bank to lend money to a new business. Borrowing from a friend or family member (or using your own savings) can be a useful <u>alternative</u>.

- <u>Mortgages</u> are long-term loans (usually more than <u>five years</u>) used to finance buying <u>property</u>. The property is used as <u>collateral</u>. Interest payments are <u>relatively low</u> compared to other borrowing types. A <u>sole trader</u> might <u>remortgage</u> their house to borrow money from the bank. The house acts as collateral — so this can be <u>risky</u>.

Don't take it too hard darling, I'm a venture capitalist — this is just what I do

5) VENTURE CAPITAL is money invested by individuals or businesses who <u>specialise</u> in giving finance to new or expanding small firms. In return they often take a <u>stake</u> in the ownership of the business. The 'dragons' on the BBC TV series Dragons' Den are examples of <u>venture capitalists</u>.

For <u>new</u> and <u>small</u> firms, it can be <u>hard</u> to raise finance.

- These firms probably won't make huge <u>profits</u>, so they won't have much <u>spare cash</u> to <u>fund</u> new projects.

- This can make banks and other lenders <u>reluctant</u> to lend money to them — compared to larger firms, there's a greater <u>risk</u> that they won't be able to <u>repay</u> the loan.

## Start-up capital — every start-up country needs one...

Lots of <u>facts</u> on this page — make sure you can write down every <u>source of finance</u> for a small firm and try to remember one <u>problem</u> with each. Learn, cover the page and start scribbling.

# Starting a Business — Help and Support

Starting a new business isn't easy — even if you've done GCSE Business Studies.
You need to know what help is available and why so many organisations are keen to help.

## The Government Gives A Lot of Help

1) The government has a lot to gain by encouraging new businesses. Many people start businesses as an alternative to unemployment. This reduces the amount of state benefits the government has to pay out.

2) The government will also receive taxation revenue when the firm makes a profit. And successful businesses create employment for many people — helping both themselves and the government even more.

3) The government funds Business Link, which operates in each region and offers help and support to businesses. It provides guidance on things like how to produce a business plan, as well as more general information like advice on staff training.

4) Another body providing help is the government's Department for Business, Enterprise and Regulatory Reform (BERR) — it provides advice and leaflets, most of which are available on its website.

5) New firms can also apply to have bank loans underwritten by the government. This means the government will pay the money back if the business fails — making it easier for the new firm to borrow money.

> Prosthetic Limbs Inc.
>
> I just need a hand – a bit of a leg-up to get me started.

## Private Firms also Offer Support

1) The most obvious examples are banks. They help new businesses by:

- Offering financial support in the form of overdrafts and loans.
- Giving new businesses advice on how to manage their finances, calculate taxes and keep records. Many banks have small business advisors to talk to potential entrepreneurs and offer them advice.
- Sometimes they will put new businesses in contact with suppliers or potential customers.

2) Banks do this for two main reasons. Firstly, to get the firm to open an account with them and not with one of their competitors. And secondly, to reduce the chances of the new business going bankrupt owing the bank lots of money.

3) Some firms exist to provide management services to other businesses — they charge for their help but sometimes provide free advice to new firms. This is because they hope the new firm will pay for their services once it is established.

## A Few Charities Offer Advice and Money

1) Some charities help people start new businesses. These charities are usually started by people who believe that it is good for society to have lots of new firms starting up.

2) The most well known example is the Prince's Trust. The Prince of Wales set it up when he realised there were limited employment opportunities for young people living in inner-city areas. The charity gives advice, grants and low-interest loans to young entrepreneurs.

## Chambers of Commerce Give Help to Local Firms

Chambers of Commerce are groups of business people in a city or town who work together to look after the interests of local businesses. They provide information and support for small companies and act as an important link between local businesses and local and central government.

## I'll get by with a little help from the Chamber of Commerce...

With all that help around it's a wonder that businesses ever fail. But they do. And to make sure that you don't do likewise, you need to make sure that you learn who wants to help new businesses and why. Triffic.

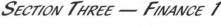

# Cash Flow

A <u>cash flow forecast</u> shows all the money that's <u>coming into</u> and <u>going out of</u> a business. Quite a <u>handy</u> thing for a business to know, and also GCSE Business Studies students as it happens....

## Cash Flow is More Than Just Profits

*The cash flow's good today.*

1) <u>Cash flow</u> is the flow of all money <u>into</u> and <u>out of</u> the business. When a firm <u>sells its products</u>, money flows in (<u>cash inflow</u>). When it buys materials or pays wages, money flows out (<u>cash outflow</u>). It's a bit like water flowing into a bath through the tap and out through the plughole.

2) <u>Net cash flow</u> is the <u>difference</u> between <u>cash inflow</u> and <u>cash outflow</u> over a period of time.

3) Cash flow's important because if there's <u>not enough</u> money flowing <u>in</u>, you don't have enough to <u>pay your bills</u>.

## Cash Flow Forecasts Help Firms to Anticipate Problems

1) A <u>cash flow forecast</u> is a good way of <u>predicting</u> when the firm might face a <u>liquidity problem</u> (lack of cash). It lists all the <u>inflows</u> and <u>outflows</u> of cash that appear in the <u>budget</u>.

2) The firm will see when an <u>overdraft</u> or other short-term finance might be needed.

3) The forecast needs to be <u>watched carefully</u> — to monitor the impact of <u>unexpected cash flows</u>.

Businesses <u>forecast</u> their <u>sales volume</u> to estimate what their <u>revenue</u> will be (over a given period of time) — these predictions are often based on sales from <u>previous</u> months or years, and the firm's best <u>guess</u>.

### Cash Flow Forecast — Footy Fanzines Ltd.

|  | April | May | June | July | August | Sept |
|---|---|---|---|---|---|---|
| Total receipts (cash inflow) | 15,000 | 12,000 | 5000 | 5000 | 16,000 | 16,000 |
| Total spending (cash outflow) | 12,000 | 12,000 | 10,000 | 10,000 | 12,000 | 12,000 |
| Net cash flow (inflow – outflow) | 3000 | 0 | -5000 | -5000 | 4000 | 4000 |
| Bank balance at start of month | 1000 | 4000 | 4000 | -1000 | -6000 | -2000 |
| Bank balance at end of month | 4000 | 4000 | -1000 | -6000 | -2000 | 2000 |

bank balance at <u>end</u> of month = bank balance at <u>start</u> of month + net cash flow

1) Here's an example of a <u>cash flow forecast</u> for a firm publishing football magazines.

2) In June and July, when the football season's over, the <u>net cash flow</u> is negative because more money flows <u>out</u> than <u>in</u>.

3) The firm can see it will need an <u>overdraft</u> to get it through from June to September.

4) It's useful to know this <u>in advance</u> because it means the firm can <u>plan</u> — it won't suddenly have to <u>panic</u> in June when it starts to <u>run out of money</u>.

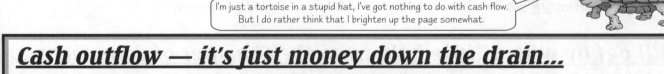

I'm just a tortoise in a stupid hat, I've got nothing to do with cash flow. But I do rather think that I brighten up the page somewhat.

## Cash outflow — it's just money down the drain...

Cash flow is quite easy — once you've understood how the <u>figures</u> are worked out. Make sure you can understand the figures in that <u>table</u>, and that you know <u>why</u> cash flow is <u>important</u>.

# Cash Flow — Credit

A firm's cash flow will <u>change</u> if they give their customers <u>longer to pay</u> for products — called <u>credit</u>.

## Credit Terms Can Affect Cash Flow

<u>Credit terms</u> tell you how long after <u>agreeing</u> to buy a product the customer has to <u>pay</u>.
This can affect the <u>timings</u> of their cash flows.

1) Stuffin's Turkeys Ltd. <u>sell most</u> of their products in <u>December</u>.

2) This table assumes customers <u>pay</u> when they <u>purchase</u> the product.

> I'm up for Turkey in December.

### Cash Flow Forecast — Stuffin's Turkeys Ltd.

|  | October | November | December | January | February | March |
|---|---|---|---|---|---|---|
| Total receipts (cash inflow) | 800 | 1500 | 12000 | 300 | 500 | 300 |
| Total payments (cash outflow) | 3000 | 4000 | 2000 | 300 | 200 | 150 |
| Net cash flow | -2200 | -2500 | 10000 | 0 | 300 | 150 |
| Bank balance at start of month | 3000 | 800 | -1700 | 8300 | 8300 | 8600 |
| Bank balance at end of month | 800 | -1700 | 8300 | 8300 | 8600 | 8750 |

3) This table assumes customers are given <u>60 days credit</u> to pay.

4) It's a bit more <u>complicated</u> as the total receipts come in <u>two months</u> after the sale is made.

### Cash Flow Forecast — Stuffin's Turkeys Ltd.

|  | October | November | December | January | February | March |
|---|---|---|---|---|---|---|
| Total sales this month (for payment in 60 days) | 800 | 1500 | 12000 | 300 | 500 | 300 |
| Total receipts (cash inflow) | 200 | 200 | 800 | 1500 | 12000 | 300 |
| Total payments (cash outflow) | 3000 | 4000 | 2000 | 300 | 200 | 150 |
| Net cash flow | -2800 | -3800 | -1200 | 1200 | 11800 | 150 |
| Bank balance at start of month | 3000 | 200 | -3600 | -4800 | -3600 | 8200 |
| Bank balance at end of month | 200 | -3600 | -4800 | -3600 | 8200 | 8350 |

*Payment made in 2 months*

> In <u>February</u>, the <u>total receipts</u> are for the turkeys bought in <u>December</u>.
> So <u>net cash flow</u> is 12000 – 200 = <u>11800</u>

5) The <u>main differences</u> are:
   • when customers pay cash there is only <u>one month</u> where <u>short-term finance</u> is needed.
   • when they pay on <u>60 days credit</u> the business will need to arrange short-term finance for <u>3 months</u>.

## Me, write a naff joke? Give me a little credit please...

Make sure you know how <u>credit terms</u> can affect a firm's cash flow. You <u>won't</u> be asked to <u>fill in</u> a cash flow forecast in your exam, but you need to be able to look at one and work out <u>what's going on</u>. What fun.

# Cash Flow — Problems

It's no use running from the truth. The sad fact is that a lot of firms go bust sooner or later. And more profitable businesses go bankrupt because of poor cash flow than for any other reason.

## Poor Cash Flow Means You've Got Big Problems

1) Poor cash flow means there is not enough cash in the business to meet its day-to-day expenses — there is a lack of working capital.

2) Staff may not get paid on time — this will cause resentment and poor motivation.

3) Some suppliers offer discounts for prompt payment of invoices — the business will not be able to take advantage of these.

4) Creditors (people or firms that are owed money) may not get paid on time — they may insist on stricter credit terms in future.

5) Some creditors may not wait for payment — they might take legal action to recover the debt. If the business does not have the money it may go into receivership (a 'receiver' is appointed to reclaim money owed to the creditors by selling off a struggling firm's assets) or be forced to cease trading.

## There are Three Main Reasons for Poor Cash Flow...

Our new line of sandpaper beachwear hasn't sold as well as we'd hoped.

1) **POOR SALES** There's a lack of demand from consumers for the firm's products, so the firm has less money coming in and it cannot pay its creditors.

2) **OVERTRADING** The firm takes on too many orders — as a result it buys in too many raw materials and hires too many staff. Something goes wrong with the orders and the firm doesn't get the money from its customers quickly enough to pay its debts.

3) **POOR BUSINESS DECISIONS** — for example the firm decides to bring out new products or expand into new markets but they do not bring in as much money as forecast. Bad business decisions are usually caused by not doing enough planning or market research.

## ...and Three Ways Businesses Can Improve Cash Flow

1) A business could "reschedule their receipts of income". For example they could give their customers less generous credit terms or insist they pay cash.

2) They could try to reschedule the payments they make to their suppliers. This could include negotiating better credit terms — ideally, the credit period given to customers should be less than the credit period obtained from suppliers.

3) Most firms carry a stock of unsold products — they could simply sell these instead of making more.
   - By destocking, the cash inflows will be the same — but cash outflows will be reduced as less will be spent on raw materials.
   - However, eventually they'll run out of stock. At this point, they'll have to start paying out money to make more products.

## Poor cash flow — best get a plumber in...

Make sure you know the problems associated with poor cash flow, why a firm may have poor cash flow, and what they can do to improve it. Once you've nailed that, it's onwards to another fabulous revision summary.

# Revision Summary for Section Three

It's that time again, I'm afraid — time to check you've learned all the stuff in this section. I know it's a pain but believe me it's worth it. Finance is really important to small businesses so that means it's important to you as well. You can almost guarantee it'll come up somehow or other in your exam. So no slacking — get your nose to the grindstone and check you can answer these questions. (Numerical answers are at the bottom of the page.)

1) List three examples of direct costs. And three examples of indirect costs.

2) Define each of the following terms:
   a) Sales
   b) Price
   c) Revenue
   d) Costs

3) If Tardy Ltd. output 30,000 alarm clocks at a total cost of £120,000, what is the average cost of making each clock?

4) Calculate how much profit a business made in 2008 if it had revenue of £125,000 and costs of £80,000.

5) If a firm's revenue is lower than its costs over a period of time, will the firm make a profit or a loss?

6) Give two reasons why a new business needs a source of start-up finance.

7) Name two short-term sources of finance, and explain how they work.

8) Describe one benefit for a business of using a grant over other sources of start-up finance.

9) Explain what is meant by venture capital.

10) Why might a new or small firm find it hard to raise finance?

11) Explain two ways that the government helps new businesses.

12) Describe how it may be beneficial to banks to help new businesses.
    Give two examples of ways that they do this.

13) Explain how the Prince's Trust helps young entrepreneurs.

14) Explain what each of the following terms mean:
    a) Cash inflow
    b) Cash outflow
    c) Net cash flow

15) Explain why a cash flow forecast is useful to a business.

16) A firm started the month with a bank balance of £2500 and had a net cash flow of £3000 for the month. What was the firm's bank balance at the end of the month?

17) What do credit terms tell you?

18) Explain how letting customers pay for goods on credit can affect a firm's cash flow.

19) Dave's Dodgy Motors Ltd. is suffering from poor cash flow. Explain three problems that might result.

20) Explain how overtrading can lead to poor cash flow.

21) Give three ways that a business could try to improve its cash flow.

22) Drink some tea before starting Section Four.

# Recruitment — Job Analysis

Recruitment is about appointing the <u>best person</u> to do a job. There's more than one way to find candidates — the method that's used will depend on the <u>business</u> and the <u>type of job</u> that's on offer.

## Firms Should Describe the Job and the Ideal Candidate

Before advertising a job, firms think about what it <u>involves</u>, and the <u>type of person</u> they want to apply for it.

1) The <u>job description</u> explains what the job involves. It includes the <u>formal title</u> of the job, the main <u>purpose</u> of the job, and the job's <u>main duties</u>. It should also say whether the job is <u>full-time</u> or <u>part-time</u>.

> • <u>Full-time</u> staff are <u>expensive</u> to pay, but they're available for the <u>whole working week</u>.
>
> • <u>Part-time</u> workers are <u>less expensive</u> if there's not enough work to fill a full-time position. They may also be better rested and <u>more motivated</u> than staff who work 9 to 5 every day.
>
> • Some firms are <u>flexible</u> with working hours to allow staff to spend time with their families.

2) The <u>person specification</u> lists the <u>qualifications</u>, <u>experience</u> and <u>attitudes</u> the <u>ideal</u> candidate would have. Some of these criteria will be <u>essential</u> to the job, but some of them will only be <u>desirable</u>.

## Personal Recommendations Can be Useful when Recruiting

1) Some job vacancies can be filled by someone <u>personally recommended</u> by a friend or an existing worker.

2) This method is especially useful for small businesses — it <u>saves money</u> on advertising the job, and a candidate who has been recommended is more likely to <u>fit in</u> well with existing staff.

## A Job Advertisement Gets Candidates to Apply

If a business can't fill the vacancy through a personal recommendation, the job will be <u>advertised</u>.

• A firm might decide to advertise <u>internally</u> — it's <u>cheaper</u>, the post can be filled <u>more quickly</u>, and candidates will already <u>know</u> the firm well.

• On the <u>downside</u>, there will be <u>no 'new blood' and ideas</u>, and the promotion will leave a <u>vacancy</u> to fill. And in a <u>small</u> business, there may be <u>very few</u> possible candidates to choose from.

• If the job is advertised <u>externally</u>, the advert will be seen by a <u>wider range</u> of applicants.

• Possible locations include <u>local and national press</u>, <u>job centres</u>, <u>trade journals</u>, <u>recruitment websites</u> and <u>employment agencies</u> (see below).

• Usually, only <u>highly-paid</u> or <u>specialist</u> jobs are advertised in the national press — it's much more <u>expensive</u> than the local press.

## Human Resources and Agencies Can Also Find Candidates

1) Some firms have a <u>human resources</u> (<u>HR</u>) department that looks after the <u>people</u> who work for the firm.

2) Part of the HR department's job is to organise <u>recruitment</u> — this includes producing <u>job descriptions</u> and <u>job advertisements</u>.

> I'll be honest with you, Alan — this isn't really what we had in mind.

3) Some companies also use <u>agencies</u> to help them find job candidates. These are separate businesses that <u>specialise</u> in finding people who match the job description.

4) <u>Headhunters</u> may also be used — these people seek out candidates who work for <u>other businesses</u>. Headhunters are <u>expensive</u> to hire, so they're usually only used to fill highly-paid <u>senior</u> positions.

## Lonely business WLTM right person for ~~cuddles~~ hard graft...

Recruitment is like love. You decide what <u>type of person</u> you're looking for, and how much <u>time</u> you want to commit. Then you put an <u>advert</u> in the newspaper and prepare for disappointment. Just like love, right?

# Recruitment — the Selection Process

Businesses usually like to have a <u>number</u> of candidates when they're trying to fill a vacancy.
The selection process then helps <u>compare</u> these candidates and decide which one is <u>best</u> for the job.

## Candidates Explain Why They're Right for the Job

Once they've found their candidates, businesses usually ask them to send a <u>written application</u> for a job.

1) A <u>curriculum vitae (CV)</u> is a summary of a person's personal details, skills, qualifications and interests. It's written in a <u>standard format</u> to give the firm the basic <u>facts</u>. Almost <u>all</u> firms ask for a CV.

2) Many businesses also ask candidates to fill in an <u>application form</u>. These forms give the firm the information it wants — and <u>nothing else</u>. This means they're much <u>quicker</u> to process and more <u>relevant</u> to the job than open-ended letters written by the candidates.

3) Some companies now like to use <u>online</u> application forms, where applicants fill in their details on the company's website. This allows the company to <u>compare</u> the applications using computer software.

<u>Shortlisted</u> candidates will usually be asked for <u>references</u>. These are statements about the character of the candidate written by someone who knows them — often a previous <u>line manager</u>.

References are usually <u>confidential</u> — the candidate won't see what's written about them.

## An Interview is the Traditional Selection Method

1) Once the closing date for applications has passed, managers in the business make a <u>shortlist</u> of the best applicants. Shortlisted candidates are invited for an <u>interview</u> with at least one manager.

2) Interviewers should ask the <u>same questions</u> to <u>all candidates</u> so that the process is <u>fair</u>. They shouldn't ask questions that are <u>irrelevant</u> to the job or that unfairly <u>discriminate</u>.

3) Interviews are used to assess a candidate's <u>confidence</u>, their <u>social</u> and <u>verbal skills</u>, and whether they'll be <u>compatible</u> with existing workers. Businesses also want to find out about the candidate's general <u>attitude</u>.

4) Some people think that interviews are <u>not a good way</u> to select — people don't behave <u>naturally</u> in a formal interview. The skills needed to be good at interview are often <u>different</u> from the skills needed to do the job.

*Sorry. I can never behave naturally at interviews.*

## Tests Can Also Help Select Who to Employ

1) Some businesses use <u>tests</u> — these are better than interviews for assessing the skills needed <u>for the job</u>. They can also be useful for spotting <u>differences</u> between <u>similar</u> candidates. There are four main types:

- <u>Skills tests</u> or <u>in-tray exercises</u> test whether the candidate has the <u>abilities</u> to do the job.
- <u>Aptitude tests</u> find out whether the candidate has the <u>potential</u> to learn how to do the job.
- <u>Personality tests</u> such as handwriting analysis are used to assess the candidate's <u>personal qualities</u>.
- <u>Group tests</u> find out whether the candidate can work as part of a team — and whether they have good <u>leadership</u> and <u>decision-making skills</u>.

2) When all the candidates have been assessed, managers and HR staff meet to discuss how well the candidates have done. They then <u>select</u> the best candidates and offer them jobs.

## Sick of recruitment methods? No need to get testy...

Businesses can often get <u>hundreds</u> of applications for one job. Choosing between all the candidates can be a <u>major task</u> — reading <u>application forms</u>, conducting <u>interviews</u> and setting <u>tests</u> takes time and money.

# Financial Rewards

There are a lot of facts on this page but it all boils down to two things
— the different ways of paying people and the incentives each method gives them.

## Workers Can be Paid Wages or a Salary

1) Wages are usually paid to manual workers — they change depending on the amount of work done.

> A time rate pays workers by the hour. It encourages people to work long hours — the problem is they also have an incentive to work slowly. Time rate is best for jobs where measuring output is difficult — like driving a bus.

> A piece rate is used if the output of each worker can be easily measured (such as a worker who sews sleeves onto shirts in a factory). Piece rates encourage people to work quickly — but if they work too fast, quality may suffer.

2) A salary is a fixed amount paid every month. It is usually paid to office staff who do not directly help to make the product. A salary of £24,000 means you are paid £2000 per month.

3) The advantage of a salary is that the firm and workers both know exactly how much the pay will be. But pay stays the same no matter how well staff perform — it doesn't reward improved performance.

## Employers Can Give Staff Extra Payments

1) With performance-related pay (PRP) the amount employees earn depends on how well they work.

> Commission is often paid to sales staff. They earn a small basic salary and then earn more money for every item they sell.

> A bonus is a lump sum added to pay, usually once a year. It's paid if the worker has met their performance targets.

2) Some businesses offer a pension scheme. The business makes payments into a pension fund each month, as long as the employee also pays money into the fund. This encourages staff to save for retirement.

## Employees are Paid What They're Worth to the Business

1) In most businesses, different staff will be given different pay.

2) Jobs that need a lot of skills and qualifications usually pay more than unskilled jobs. The age and experience of the worker can also have an effect — most people earn more as they get older and progress through their careers.

> We've decided that you're worth... jack. Congratulations.

3) Managers have to work out how much each employee is worth to the business and pay them a suitable wage or salary.

## Temporary Workers can Help With Short-Term Tasks

> Fear not — Captain Freelance is here to sort out your filing.

1) Temporary staff are paid for a fixed period of a few weeks or months. Employment agencies often supply firms with temporary staff — for a fee.

2) Freelance workers are also temporary — but they're usually self-employed. A business might bring them in to help with a particular task.

3) These types of staff give businesses flexibility — they can get extra staff for a short time according to the work that needs to be done.

4) Sometimes temporary staff are paid more than permanent employees to make up for the lack of job security — and to give them an extra incentive to work hard.

## Financial rewards — I'm in it for the money, innit?

Staff can be paid wages or a salary — but businesses give the highest pay to the employees that are most valuable to the company. Workers can also be given extra financial perks like bonuses and pension payments.

# Non-Financial Rewards

Businesses need to keep their staff <u>motivated</u> (see page 66). Paying workers well and giving them other financial rewards can help their motivation, but businesses can reward their staff without spending more cash.

## Motivated Staff are Good for Business

You might ask why businesses are so keen to keep their staff motivated in the first place. Well...

1) Motivated workers <u>perform better</u>. They'll produce more and better-quality products.

2) They'll also <u>stay</u> with the company for <u>longer</u>, reducing <u>staff turnover</u> — this <u>saves money</u> since the business spends less on recruiting and training new workers.

## Training Can Boost Motivation...

Employees can become <u>bored</u> and <u>frustrated</u> if they're stuck with the same task for a long time. Businesses can help to keep their staff motivated by offering them <u>training</u>.

1) Training can <u>improve motivation</u> as it makes people better at their jobs, and people usually enjoy being <u>good</u> at what they're doing.

2) Employees can also be trained to learn <u>new skills</u>. This means they can start to take on <u>new tasks</u>.

## Giving Staff More Responsibility Can be Motivating

Sometimes giving staff <u>more variety</u> or <u>extra responsibilities</u> can help them to stay motivated.

- **JOB ENLARGEMENT** means giving a productive member of staff <u>more tasks</u> to do. This will increase the size of their <u>job description</u>.
- The extra tasks should make the job more <u>varied</u> and <u>interesting</u>. It can also make the worker feel more <u>valued</u>.

Maybe this job enlargement wasn't such a good idea.

- **JOB ENRICHMENT** involves giving a worker <u>greater responsibility</u> — for example <u>supervising</u> the work of new staff.
- This may mean the worker needs more <u>training</u> (see above), but they may become more <u>motivated</u> and <u>work harder</u>.

## Fringe Benefits — Those Extra Little Perks

This free gym membership is great. But what does the company get out of it?

OFFICE POWER GENERATOR

1) A <u>fringe benefit</u> is any reward that is not part of a worker's <u>main income</u>.

2) Examples include the use of a <u>company car</u>, <u>gym membership</u>, a daily <u>meal allowance</u> or free <u>health insurance</u>.

3) All of these perks <u>cost</u> money for the business, and <u>save</u> it for the worker — you could argue that they're types of financial reward.

- Every business has to find the most <u>appropriate</u> way to reward its staff. The rewards could be <u>financial</u>, <u>non-financial</u>, or a <u>mixture</u> of both.
- For example, a <u>small business</u> might not be able to pay its staff huge <u>salaries</u>. But giving staff extra <u>responsibility</u> may be an effective alternative.

## I asked for a fringe benefit — my boss bought me hair gel...

Whether businesses like it or not, employees are <u>people</u> too. They like to feel <u>appreciated</u> and be given <u>variety</u> and <u>responsibility</u> in their jobs. And they probably won't complain if you pay for their <u>lunch</u>, either.

# Employment and the Law

This page is crammed <u>full of facts</u> about the <u>law</u>. You don't need to know the names of any acts — just their <u>effects</u> on <u>small businesses</u>. Just learn the stuff on this page and you'll be right.

## ① Employment Rights and the Minimum Wage

1) All employees must be given a <u>written contract of employment</u> within <u>two months</u> of starting work.

2) All staff should have a copy of the business's <u>discipline procedure</u>.
   This explains which offences would lead to a <u>warning</u>, and which would lead to <u>dismissal</u>.

3) European Union law limits the working week to <u>48 hours</u> for most employees.

4) The Government sets a <u>National Minimum Wage</u> for most workers, depending on their age.
   This makes it <u>illegal</u> for businesses to pay workers <u>less</u> than this minimum amount.

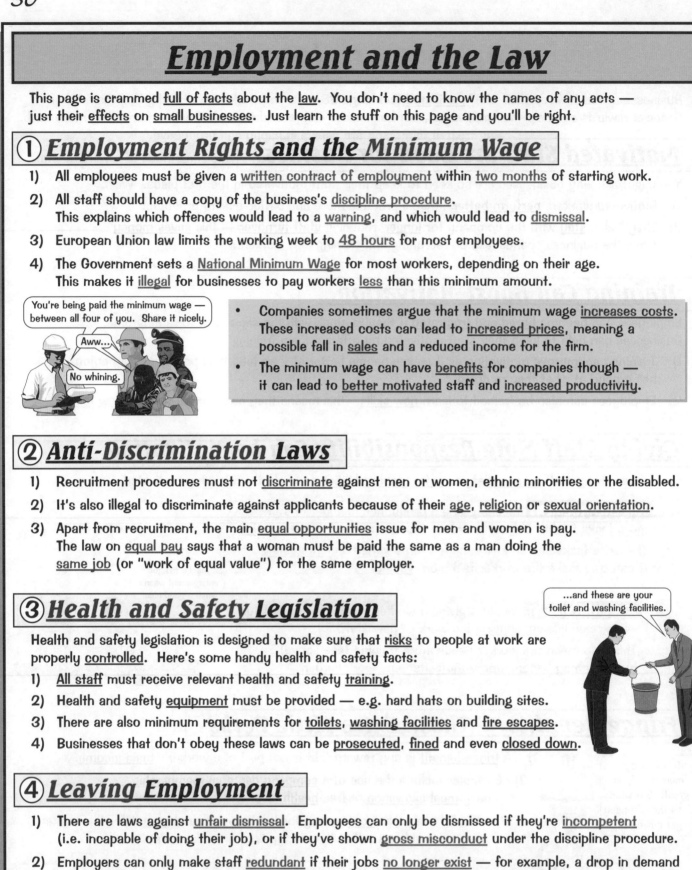

You're being paid the minimum wage — between all four of you. Share it nicely.

Aww...

No whining.

- Companies sometimes argue that the minimum wage <u>increases costs</u>. These increased costs can lead to <u>increased prices</u>, meaning a possible fall in <u>sales</u> and a reduced income for the firm.

- The minimum wage can have <u>benefits</u> for companies though — it can lead to <u>better motivated</u> staff and <u>increased productivity</u>.

## ② Anti-Discrimination Laws

1) Recruitment procedures must not <u>discriminate</u> against men or women, ethnic minorities or the disabled.

2) It's also illegal to discriminate against applicants because of their <u>age</u>, <u>religion</u> or <u>sexual orientation</u>.

3) Apart from recruitment, the main <u>equal opportunities</u> issue for men and women is pay.
   The law on <u>equal pay</u> says that a woman must be paid the same as a man doing the
   <u>same job</u> (or "work of equal value") for the same employer.

## ③ Health and Safety Legislation

...and these are your toilet and washing facilities.

Health and safety legislation is designed to make sure that <u>risks</u> to people at work are properly <u>controlled</u>. Here's some handy health and safety facts:

1) <u>All staff</u> must receive relevant health and safety <u>training</u>.

2) Health and safety <u>equipment</u> must be provided — e.g. hard hats on building sites.

3) There are also minimum requirements for <u>toilets</u>, <u>washing facilities</u> and <u>fire escapes</u>.

4) Businesses that don't obey these laws can be <u>prosecuted</u>, <u>fined</u> and even <u>closed down</u>.

## ④ Leaving Employment

1) There are laws against <u>unfair dismissal</u>. Employees can only be dismissed if they're <u>incompetent</u> (i.e. incapable of doing their job), or if they've shown <u>gross misconduct</u> under the discipline procedure.

2) Employers can only make staff <u>redundant</u> if their jobs <u>no longer exist</u> — for example, a drop in demand for a product may mean that fewer workers are needed. The firm <u>cannot re-advertise</u> a redundant job.

3) Employees who think they have been <u>unfairly</u> dismissed or made redundant can usually appeal to an <u>employment tribunal</u>. The tribunal can award <u>compensation</u> or <u>reinstate</u> the employee.

## Unfair dismissal — it clearly hit the pad, not the bat...

Keeping within the law is <u>expensive</u> — keeping up to date with new laws costs <u>money</u> and creates a lot of <u>paperwork</u> (and small firms have to meet all the same requirements as large ones, remember). But these laws are all about making sure employees (and potential employees) are treated <u>fairly</u> and can work in <u>safety</u>.

# Revision Summary for Section Four

People... can't live with them, can't fire them all.  But until the world is taken over by robots in 2032, businesses are going to need people to get anything done.  This section is about making sure that the people who work for a business are being treated fairly, and are generally happy and productive.

For this section, you need to know about recruitment, financial and non-financial methods of rewarding staff, and employment law.  And remember to keep small businesses in mind while you're at it.

You've got things to think about, then — but if you can answer all these questions, you're well on your way...

1)      Why might a business want to employ part-time staff?

2)      Why do businesses sometimes employ staff that have been personally recommended?

3)      Explain the pros and cons of advertising a job internally.

4)      Now explain the pros and cons of advertising a job externally.

5)      What (in the field of recruitment) is a 'headhunter'?

6)      Describe two written documents that people can use to say why they're the right person for a job.

7)      List three things that are assessed in a job interview.

8)      Name four types of test a firm might use to help them decide who to employ.

9)      What's the name of the pay method when workers are paid by the hour?
        Explain one advantage and one disadvantage of this pay method.

10)     What is the piece rate pay method?  Explain one advantage and one disadvantage of it.

11)     What is an advantage of paying staff a salary?

12)     Give two reasons why different staff in a business might be given different pay.

13)     Give one advantage that temporary staff can have for a business.

14)     Give two reasons why motivated staff are good for a business.

15)     Explain the difference between job enlargement and job enrichment.

16)     Give three examples of fringe benefits.

17)     Explain why non-financial rewards may be a particularly good way of motivating staff in a small business.

18)     Which of these must all employees be given within two months of starting work?
        a) a contract;  b) a pay rise;  c) the sack.

19)     What information should a business's discipline procedure give to employees?

20)     It's illegal for employers to discriminate against people because of their age.
        List four more features that it's illegal to discriminate against when selecting job candidates.

21)     What does the law say about pay for men and women working for the same employer?

22)     Describe some steps that a business must take in order to comply with health and safety legislation.

23)     In what circumstances is it legal for a business to dismiss an employee?

# Methods of Production

Most things you buy in the shops will have been <u>produced</u> by a business.  Businesses use different methods of production depending on the product — they're aiming for <u>low costs</u> and <u>high output</u>.

## Businesses Aim for Efficient Production

1) It's important for a business to operate <u>efficiently</u> — i.e. produce the <u>maximum</u> amount possible with the <u>minimum input</u> of people and raw materials.

2) An efficient business will have <u>lower operating costs</u> than an inefficient one producing the same output (maybe because fewer workers or other resources are needed).  Lower costs result in <u>higher profits</u>.

3) When it comes to <u>production</u>, achieving efficiency involves considering several different factors. For instance:

- The <u>type of product</u>:  a method that's efficient for producing pedalos probably won't be so good for making an enormous cruise liner.

- The level of <u>demand</u> for the product:  if your business sells ten silver bracelets per year, there's no point making them by the lorryload — you'd be better off keeping production runs low.

- The <u>cost</u>:  the most efficient method of production may require expensive machinery, or an increased workforce — a small business may not be able to afford to invest in this, even if it would improve the production process.

4) Businesses need to choose the best <u>method of production</u> for their situation.  A couple of possible methods are explained below.

> There's also the method of flow production (see page 69), but you don't need to know about that for this Unit.

## ① Job Production is Making One Thing at a Time

**BIBLE PRODUCTION**

When you've finished on that Job, make a start on those Psalms, will you?

Yes, sir.

1) <u>Job production</u> is used when a firm manufactures <u>individual</u> products. Each product can have a <u>unique design</u>, and can even be based upon the <u>customer's specification</u>.  If they're made in a factory, the firm may need to <u>retool</u> its factory for each new product.

2) These products often require highly <u>skilled labour</u> and have a high <u>labour-to-capital ratio</u> (i.e. lots of workers are needed, but relatively little financial investment).

3) They're usually <u>expensive</u> and take a <u>long time</u> to make. But they're also <u>high quality</u>.

4) Examples include <u>ship</u> and <u>bridge</u> building, and handmade crafts such as <u>furniture making</u> and <u>made-to-measure</u> clothes.

## ② Batch Production is Making Groups of Identical Products

1) In <u>batch production</u>, firms don't just make one product at a time — they make a <u>batch</u> of identical products.  When the batch is <u>complete</u> they reorganise and make a batch of <u>something else</u>.

2) It's suited to products that are <u>identical</u> to each other, but which are only produced in <u>limited quantities</u>, or for a limited amount of time.

3) Examples include <u>furniture</u> (where producers make a limited number of many different designs), and <u>house-building</u> (where a batch of identical houses is built on a new housing estate).

## This tip is space efficient...

<u>Efficiency</u> is important for all businesses, so I'm going to save CGP some ink by leaving some blank space in this box.  There will be <u>no</u> unnecessary words here <u>whatsoever</u>.  Not a single one.  Low costs are the key.

# New Technology in the Workplace

Before computers arrived on the scene, every day was a living hell — be thankful you missed it by being born when you were. These days computer technology makes things much easier and more productive. Usually.

## Computer Software Improves Productivity

Computers have made it possible to get more done in a shorter time.

1) In offices, word processing and desktop publishing software have made it easy to produce professional and attractive documents. Customers can be contacted almost instantly via e-mail and the internet.

2) Spreadsheet software can be used to calculate costs, produce invoices, and keep accounting records.

Computers have also improved output in other types of business. For example:

1) In manufacturing, Computer Aided Design (CAD) software can be used to create a three-dimensional computer model of the product and make instant changes to the design.

2) CAM is short for Computer Aided Manufacture — it's much more accurate than traditional methods. Both CAD and CAM can improve quality and productivity, and reduce human error.

1) In shops, electronic bar codes have made adding up customers' bills a breeze. Also, sales are recorded by a computer, and when stock falls to a pre-set amount, more is automatically ordered.

2) Tills also allow customers to pay for their shopping using a debit card instead of cash. Funds are transferred directly from the customer's account to the shop's.

## Computers Reduce Costs and Increase Efficiency

1) Introducing new computer software can be a good way to increase a business's efficiency. Although initial costs can be high, it often saves time and money in the long run.

2) Many businesses have a network of linked computers. This means information can be stored on a central server and accessed by any member of staff quickly and easily.

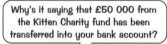

Why's it saying that £50 000 from the Kitten Charity fund has been transferred into your bank account?

Strange... must be some kind of computer error.

3) Computers are also accurate. Human brains make mistakes — cold, hard computer logic doesn't. Unfortunately, it's still possible for people to give computers the wrong information. And PCs can still crash.

4) Computer technology is improving all the time — it can be hard for businesses to keep up. Firms need to choose the technology that will benefit them most, or risk being left behind.

## Entrepreneurs Can Take Advantage of Technology

For richer, for p...

BEEP. BEEP. BEEP.

*Sigh*. Sorry, darling — I have to take this.

1) Mobile technology such as laptops and smartphones enable entrepreneurs to keep in touch with work, even while they're away from the office (at home, on the train, on their honeymoon).

2) Computers allow small businesses to automate tasks that could previously have taken several people a number of days — e.g. sending out marketing material to all previous customers. This can lead to big cost savings.

3) Specialist software also allows people with little technical expertise to master a whole range of tasks — such as producing professional-looking documents, managing their finances, setting up websites, and so on.

## This book has encountered an error and needs to close...

Bad news — in your exam, you'll probably have to use a pen. It's tough, I know, but at least you'll only get RSI in one wrist. Computers are generally great for business, but human error can still cause problems.

# Quality Assurance

Even the most productive business in the world won't get far if its products <u>aren't up to scratch</u>.
Say you buy a brand of jeans, and they turn out to be held together with staples which cut your legs to shreds
— the chances are that you won't go back and buy the same brand again.  Unless you like that sort of thing.

## Customers Expect Quality from All Parts of a Business

1)   The <u>product</u> should be good quality, of course.  More on this below...

2)   <u>Customer service</u> (see page 35) also needs to be good.  Customers expect a high standard
of service — businesses that deliver this usually do better than those that don't.

3)   Even the quality of <u>promotional material</u> can make a difference — customers may be put
off a company if one of their adverts is full of spelling mistakes, for example.

4)   <u>Quality assurance</u> is a firm's attempt to satisfy customers by making sure that quality
standards are agreed and met throughout the organisation.

## Products Should be Good Quality for their Price

1)   The <u>quality</u> of a product can depend on different factors.  For example:

> • The <u>materials</u> the product is made from.
> • The <u>production method</u> used to assemble the product (e.g. hand-crafted or mass-produced).

2)   At the very least, customers expect products to <u>work properly</u>, and <u>not fall apart</u> straight away.

3)   Good-quality products are usually made from more expensive <u>materials</u>.
Customers are often prepared to pay a <u>higher price</u> for better quality products
— as long as they're still good <u>value for money</u>.

4)   That doesn't mean that businesses can sell poor-quality products
as long as they're cheap.  In fact, it's <u>illegal</u> to sell products that
aren't of a <u>satisfactory quality</u> (see page 36).

*Reduced! Was £8.99 Now £1.50!!*

## Customers May Need Reassurance Before They Buy

Customers want <u>good quality</u> products and services.  So firms will want to make it clear to customers
that <u>they</u> can provide that good quality.  Here are a couple of ways they might go about it...

<u>QUALITY AWARDS</u> are evidence of high standards.  An example is <u>BS 5750</u>, which
the <u>British Standards Institution</u> gives to firms with good quality assurance systems.

*Quality Award 1987*

• <u>TRADE ASSOCIATIONS</u> — membership of certain <u>trade associations</u> (e.g. Federation of
Master Builders) can signify that the firm meets particular <u>standards</u> of <u>workmanship</u>.

• Belonging to a trade association may also mean that firms have to abide by a <u>code of practice</u>
(this might mean the firm has to offer a particular level of <u>customer service</u>, or <u>guarantee</u> its work).

• And if there's a <u>dispute</u> between a firm and a customer, there's someone to <u>complain</u> to.
The trade association can investigate and, if the firm has behaved badly, it can be <u>expelled</u>.

1)   Firms often display which <u>quality awards</u> they've earned, or which <u>trade associations</u> they belong
to on their <u>advertising</u>.

2)   It's a way to help <u>reassure</u> potential customers, and make them <u>more likely</u> to buy from a firm.

## Another quality tip from CGP...

It's a tough old world in business — the <u>customer</u> is king, and they expect <u>satisfaction</u>.  No business can
afford to let down its customers, and definitely not a small one — they might not get a second chance.

# Customer Service

All businesses <u>love</u> their customers. But like any relationship, things can get rocky from time to time. If you don't give your customers the right <u>service</u>, they might just lose their patience and dump you. Next time you see them, they could be snuggled up with a different brand. Heartbreaking.

## Good Customer Service — Six Examples to Learn

1) <u>Accurate product information</u>: A business should know its products inside-out, and give its customers honest information about them.

2) <u>Reliability</u>: Products need to be reliable — customers don't want to have to keep phoning a helpline because their vacuum cleaner explodes every two weeks. The <u>customer service</u> also needs to be <u>reliable</u> — e.g. you'd expect to have your call answered and the problem resolved every time you phone a helpline.

> Yes... it happened again...

3) <u>Dealing with customer questions and concerns</u> when buying a product. For example, a customer might need to be shown how a new product works.

> Er... did you order a tuxedo, mister?

4) <u>Fulfilling the order requirements</u>: If the order is for a ham and cheese pizza, don't send the customer a wooden spoon and a tube of toothpaste.

5) <u>Delivering on time</u>: If you've <u>promised</u> next-day delivery, deliver the <u>next day</u>. Don't turn up three weeks later saying you overslept.

6) <u>After-sales support and warranties</u>: Sometimes things go wrong, leading to customer questions and complaints — a good business will put the problem right. Some products, like cars and computers, might need to be serviced and updated throughout their lifespan.

Many businesses have a customer service <u>department</u> — others train <u>all staff</u> to provide a good level of customer service. Some businesses do <u>both</u>. Company <u>websites</u> can also provide customer service — see page 38 for more information.

## Good Customer Service has Benefits for a Business

1) Good customer service leads to high levels of <u>customer satisfaction</u>. Satisfied customers are more likely to make <u>repeat purchases</u> from the business in the future.

2) Happy customers are also more likely to <u>recommend</u> the business to their friends and family. <u>Word-of-mouth</u> recommendation is a very important way for a business to expand. This is especially true for small businesses.

> I caught the crocodile for you, madam. As you can see, I lost some of my clothes in the fight.

3) If customers aren't satisfied, they won't come back. The business then has to <u>work harder</u> to find <u>new</u> customers. Unhappy customers are also less likely to recommend the business to others — they might even put people off it. The business ends up with a <u>poor reputation</u> and <u>falling sales</u>.

> What excellent customer service...

PESTGO Ltd.

4) Of course, good customer service <u>costs money</u> — e.g. the wages of extra staff, and website running costs. For a small business, these costs may be a major part of their spending. But customer service is <u>crucial</u> — most businesses recognise that the <u>benefits</u> of customer service <u>outweigh</u> the costs.

## The tennis company failed — their service was broken...

If a business wants to <u>keep</u> its customers, it needs to provide them with good service. Make sure you can explain <u>why</u> customer service is important, and list the <u>different ways</u> a company can provide it.

# Government Policy — Consumer Protection

There are laws <u>restricting</u> how firms <u>sell their products</u> — the aim is to <u>protect the consumer</u>.
If these laws weren't in place, some businesses might be tempted to be <u>a bit dishonest</u>.
Like the time I bought a new TV that turned out to be an egg-whisk. Oh, come on — we've all done it.

## Sale of Goods Legislation Sets Conditions for Products

There are various laws that cover how goods and services can be sold.
They basically state that goods should meet <u>three criteria</u>:

1) **The product should be <u>fit for its purpose</u>.**

   • The product has to <u>do the job</u> it was <u>designed</u> for
   — if you buy a bucket, say, it's not much use if it leaks water out of the bottom.

2) **The product should <u>match its description</u>.**

   • It's <u>illegal</u> for a retailer to give a <u>false description</u> of something being sold.

   • This includes the <u>size</u> or <u>quantity</u> of the product, the <u>materials</u> it's made from, and its <u>properties</u>.

   • It's also illegal to claim that a product has been <u>endorsed</u> or <u>approved</u> by a person or an organization unless it really has been.

...and it's magic and fires lasers and does your maths homework and makes you really attractive...

3) **The product should be of <u>satisfactory quality</u>.**

   • This means that the product should be <u>well made</u> — it shouldn't fall apart after a couple of uses.

   • It also means that it shouldn't cause <u>other problems</u> for the buyer — e.g. a <u>fridge</u> should keep food <u>cold</u>, but it shouldn't make a <u>noise</u> like a jet plane at the same time.

Are you sure this is a size 10? It feels a bit loose...

For example, a pair of <u>size ten leather shoes</u> should be:
• the <u>right shape</u> for human feet to fit into (fit for purpose),
• <u>size ten</u> and <u>made from leather</u> (that's what the description says),
• <u>of a satisfactory quality</u> — they shouldn't fall to bits after a half-mile walk.

## Consumer Protection Laws Affect Businesses

1) Businesses have to be <u>very careful</u> when selling products and services to their customers.

2) If products don't meet the legal requirements, customers can ask for their <u>money back</u>, a <u>repair</u> or a <u>replacement</u>. This ends up costing the business money, and harms its <u>reputation</u>.

3) For small businesses, it's vital to sell <u>good quality</u> products in an <u>honest</u> way — it's basic customer service. If they don't do this, their customers will shop elsewhere — and there could be <u>legal problems</u>, too.

## Idon'tthinkmykeyboard'sspacebarisfitforitspurpose...

The gist of this page is that products need to meet a basic standard of <u>quality</u> before they can be sold. Businesses also have to <u>describe</u> their products <u>accurately</u>. If they don't, they're breaking the law and upsetting customers. Businesses don't want unhappy customers, so they need to get this stuff right.

# New Technology — E-Commerce

Since the mid 1990s the internet has led to <u>massive changes</u> in the way businesses market products. <u>Buying</u> and <u>selling</u> products and services online is called <u>e-commerce</u>.

## E-Commerce can Reduce Costs and Increase Sales

E-commerce has some big advantages over traditional methods of doing business — mostly to do with reducing <u>costs</u> and <u>prices</u>, and becoming more <u>competitive</u>.

1) E-commerce saves money on <u>paper</u>. Things like <u>sales brochures</u> and <u>product information</u> no longer need to be printed and posted by the firm — they can be viewed online or downloaded by the customer.

Download complete.

Oof.

2) Some firms employ lots of staff to <u>give out information</u> over the <u>telephone</u> — e.g. airlines and bus companies. These companies may decide to <u>save money</u> by making some of those people <u>redundant</u> and putting the information <u>online</u> instead.

3) Businesses that sell online don't need to have High Street <u>shops</u> — they can sell directly from a warehouse. This saves the business money on <u>property</u> costs.

4) It might also be possible for firms to <u>locate in more remote areas</u> where wages tend to be lower.

5) All these savings mean that e-commerce firms can offer <u>lower prices</u> than High Street shops — this is one of the main reasons that <u>sales</u> from many internet shopping sites are <u>increasing</u>.

## E-Commerce Can Reach International Markets

Another benefit of e-commerce is that it provides more <u>places</u> to sell products.

Derek Bossman's foolproof e-commerce strategy.

1) The internet can be accessed <u>all over the world</u>. As part of its <u>marketing strategy</u>, a business may want to target markets in <u>foreign countries</u> with online promotions.

2) Even <u>small companies</u> can do this, since it's much <u>cheaper</u> than buying advertising space in foreign media.

3) For all businesses, selling to international markets may lead to <u>higher profits</u>.

## Buying Online Has Pros and Cons for Consumers

A big part of e-commerce is <u>internet shopping</u> — and it's getting bigger all the time...

See the next page for more on websites.

### INTERNET SHOPPING — BENEFITS TO CONSUMERS

1) You can shop from home at <u>any</u> time, and search quickly through a huge range of <u>stock</u>.

2) It's easy to look at several sites to <u>compare</u> products and prices offered by different firms.

3) <u>Encryption software</u> means that credit card details can be sent <u>securely</u> on many websites.

4) It's often possible to <u>track the progress</u> of an order so that you know when it's likely to be delivered.

### INTERNET SHOPPING — PROBLEMS FOR CONSUMERS

1) It's often impossible to tell whether a website belongs to a <u>trustworthy</u> firm (see next page).

2) There's a chance that <u>credit or debit card details</u> could be used by others illegally.

3) Products <u>can't be seen</u> before buying, and it takes <u>time</u> for them to be delivered.

4) If goods are <u>unsuitable</u>, it can be difficult to exchange them, or get your money back.

5) Customers tend to receive lots of <u>direct e-mail</u> — advertising new products, sales etc.

## Customers always click with internet shopping...

Thanks to e-commerce, customers don't have to <u>wait</u> for the shops to open to buy the products they want. Businesses are happy too — their <u>costs</u> are coming down, and they can sell to customers across the world.

# New Technology — E-Commerce

A good website can provide customer service and technical support, or help with a firm's marketing.
But there are potential downsides too...

## Websites Can Provide Customer Services

1) Many firms include 24-hour <u>online ordering</u> on their websites, making it <u>easier</u> for customers to buy.

**Blameless Ltd. — FAQs**
Q: Why can't I speak to a real person?
A: People exhale the greenhouse gas <u>carbon dioxide</u>. This goes against our environmental policy.

2) Many sites provide answers to <u>frequently-asked questions</u> (FAQs), contact details, and provide online forms that customers can use to make enquiries or complain.

3) Some companies also let customers set up an online <u>customer account</u>. This allows customers to <u>access services</u> on the web (for example, bank websites let their customers pay bills online, mobile phone companies let customers top up their calling credit, and so on and so on).

4) Websites can also be used for <u>technical support</u> — many computer companies offer <u>updates</u> for software and hardware over the internet.

## Running a Website Can be Expensive

There are plenty of benefits to a firm of selling through its own website, but it's <u>not completely straightforward</u>.

1) Setting up and running the facilities needed for e-commerce can be <u>expensive</u> and <u>time-consuming</u>.

- New <u>equipment</u> may need to be bought and installed, and staff might need to be <u>trained</u> in using it.
- A <u>specialist website designer</u> may be needed to make the company's website attractive and accessible.
- Somebody will need to <u>update</u> the website regularly — old information is no use to customers.

2) For small businesses, these costs may not be so large — in theory, <u>anyone</u> with a computer and internet access can set up their own website. Larger businesses are likely to need more specialist staff.

## Gaining Trust is Important for Firms that Use E-Commerce

1) Company websites can be incredibly useful — they can have real benefits for <u>customers</u> and for the <u>company</u>.

2) For example, they can be updated <u>many times</u> a day — giving customers <u>up-to-date</u> information around the clock.

3) But the potential audience is <u>huge</u> — so it's <u>crucial</u> to make sure that a website <u>works</u> properly, is <u>secure</u>, and that its <u>message</u> and <u>tone</u> are right.

4) <u>Trust</u> is important on the internet. Usually the buyer has to <u>pay</u> (i.e. hand over their credit card details to the firm) <u>before</u> they get their hands on any goods.

Hi! I'm Patrick McPop-Up — don't be alarmed by my empty eyes. Click on <u>this link</u> to check out my website. I'm not trying to sell you anything, honest.

5) <u>One</u> bad experience for a customer (especially if it involves losing credit card details) can be enough to turn them off your company <u>forever</u>.

6) As a result, <u>quality of service</u> and <u>reputation</u> are possibly even more important on the internet than usual. If a seller lets a customer down, there are usually plenty of other firms' websites a customer can use just as easily.

7) To gain trust, e-commerce firms need to build up a good <u>brand image</u> and <u>customer loyalty</u> over time.

## I just feel a real connection to this business...

With more and more people connecting to the internet, a decent website is a crucial part of a business's image. The <u>costs</u> of setting up websites can be high, but firms that don't get online risk being <u>left behind</u>. The internet offers great <u>opportunities</u> for small businesses, but it can take time for them to build <u>trust</u>.

# Revision Summary for Section Five

In case you missed the title at the start, this section has been about Operations Management. Operations are the processes that make a business tick — if these processes break down, the whole business might grind to a halt.

Operations are pretty important, then — that's why examiners like to test you on them. It's also the reason that we've thoughtfully provided you with some questions to answer on the topic. Actually, we always put questions at the end of each topic, but these ones are especially enjoyable, probably.

Have fun.

1) Explain what it means for a business to be efficient.

2) Explain three factors that a business may consider when deciding on an efficient production method.

3) Describe job production and the kind of products it's used to produce.

4) What is batch production? What kinds of products might be made using batch production?

5) Which method of production should be used in the following examples? Explain your answers.
   a) making T-shirts of varying colours and styles.
   b) building luxury cruise ships to order, so each ship is a different design.

6) List three things that a business can do with spreadsheets.

7) What are CAD and CAM, and how have they improved productivity in manufacturing?

8) Explain three ways that computerisation has made businesses more efficient.

9) Explain why the computerisation of a business doesn't lead to mistakes being completely eliminated.

10) How might a very cheap armchair and a very expensive armchair differ in terms of:
    a) the quality of materials used?
    b) the production method used?

11) "It's okay for a business to sell shoddy products as long as they're cheap."
    Explain what's misleading about this sentence.

12) What are quality awards? Give an example.

13) Explain why a business might include in its advertising the names of trade associations it belongs to.

14) Describe six examples of effective customer service.

15) What benefits does providing good customer service have for a business?

16) Explain the three criteria that all products have to satisfy
    if they're not to fall foul of sale-of-goods legislation.

17) Explain three ways that e-commerce is reducing business costs.

18) Why has e-commerce made it easier for small businesses to sell their products overseas?

19) Give two benefits and two drawbacks to a consumer of buying online.

20) Give three ways that a business can provide customer service through its website.

21) Explain why a small e-commerce business could be in trouble if its website developed technical problems.

# Growth of Firms — Internal Expansion

There are <u>two ways</u> a firm can grow — <u>internally</u>, by expanding their own activities, and <u>externally</u> (see next page for more about external expansion). It's important to learn <u>why</u> firms grow as well as <u>how</u> they grow.

## Firms Grow for Various Reasons

Here are <u>five</u> reasons why businesses might want to expand...

1) **ECONOMIES OF SCALE** Larger firms can produce at <u>lower average cost</u> (see page 71) than smaller firms. They can pass on these <u>economies of scale</u> to consumers as <u>lower prices</u>. This will help them increase their <u>sales</u>, their <u>market share</u> and their <u>profits</u>.

2) **DIVERSIFICATION** Larger firms can afford to produce <u>more products</u> than smaller firms. They can sell into <u>different markets</u> and so <u>reduce the risks</u> that a decline in sales of one product will harm the business. That means there's less threat to their <u>profits</u>.

See also page 48.

3) **FINANCIAL SUPPORT** Larger firms are <u>less likely</u> to go <u>bust</u> than smaller firms. That's mainly because they can <u>borrow money</u> more easily from banks so they will find it easier to survive <u>cash flow</u> problems. Larger firms are also more likely to receive financial support from the <u>government</u> than smaller firms because they employ lots of people.

4) **PERSONAL VANITY** Some owners also enjoy the <u>power</u> and <u>status</u> that comes from owning a large business.

5) **DOMINATION OF THE MARKET** The <u>larger</u> the <u>market share</u> a firm has, the more it can <u>control</u> the price of its products. It will face <u>fewer threats</u> from competitors and may even be able to <u>eliminate</u> rivals by charging prices that they can't compete with.

## There are Three Main Methods of Internal Expansion

Internal expansion is also called <u>organic growth</u>.

1) The firm can <u>produce more</u> of its <u>current products</u> to sell in its <u>existing markets</u>. For example Glugg Soft Drinks Ltd. could try to increase its market share in the UK fizzy cabbage juice market from 1% to 20%.

2) The firm can sell its <u>current product</u> into <u>new markets</u>. Glugg Soft Drinks could try to export its fizzy cabbage juice to the USA.

3) The firm could launch a <u>new product</u>. This could be a similar product to existing ones, like fizzy turnip juice — this is called <u>line extension</u>, because you're extending your line of products. Or it could be a completely new product, like sports cars — this is an example of <u>diversification</u>.

Glugg Ltd Strategy Meeting

I've got a better idea. Let's make a sports car that runs on cabbage juice.

## Internal Expansion has its Benefits and Problems

1) Internal growth is good in that it is relatively <u>inexpensive</u> to achieve. Also, with the exception of diversifying into a completely new product, the firm expands by doing more of what it is <u>already good at</u> — making its existing products. That means it's less likely to go horribly wrong.

2) The problem is that it can take a <u>long time</u> to achieve growth. Some owners are <u>not prepared to wait</u> that long — that's why they go for external growth.

## Organic growth — expansion without pesticides...

Make sure you learn all the <u>reasons for growth</u> as well as the benefits and problems of <u>internal expansion</u>. Memorise the three types of internal expansion — then try to find some <u>examples</u> of firms that have grown in each of these ways. Don't spend too much time wondering what fizzy cabbage juice would taste like.

# Growth of Firms — External Expansion

Takeovers and mergers are the two ways to achieve external expansion. Roughly speaking, a merger is when two firms join together to form a new (but larger) firm, and a takeover is when an existing firm expands by buying another firm. Unless you're an accountant, it's sometimes hard to tell the difference, to be honest.

## External Expansion — Four Examples to Think About

There are four basic ways a firm can merge with, or take over other firms:

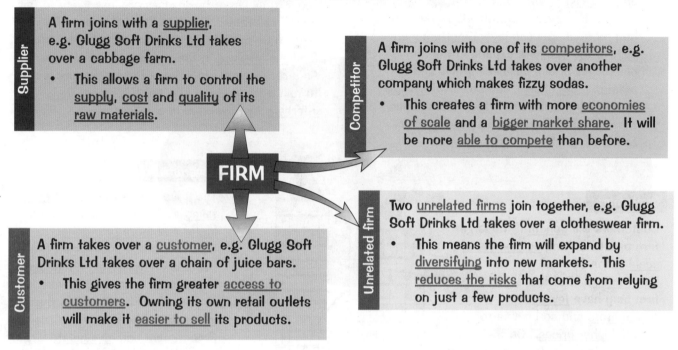

**Supplier**

A firm joins with a supplier, e.g. Glugg Soft Drinks Ltd takes over a cabbage farm.
- This allows a firm to control the supply, cost and quality of its raw materials.

**Competitor**

A firm joins with one of its competitors, e.g. Glugg Soft Drinks Ltd takes over another company which makes fizzy sodas.
- This creates a firm with more economies of scale and a bigger market share. It will be more able to compete than before.

**FIRM**

**Customer**

A firm takes over a customer, e.g. Glugg Soft Drinks Ltd takes over a chain of juice bars.
- This gives the firm greater access to customers. Owning its own retail outlets will make it easier to sell its products.

**Unrelated firm**

Two unrelated firms join together, e.g. Glugg Soft Drinks Ltd takes over a clotheswear firm.
- This means the firm will expand by diversifying into new markets. This reduces the risks that come from relying on just a few products.

## Mergers and Takeovers Don't Always Go Smoothly

1) Less than half of all takeovers and mergers are successful. It's very hard to make two different businesses work as one. Management styles often differ between firms — the employees of one firm may be used to one company culture and not be motivated by the style used in the other.

2) Mergers and takeovers can also create bad feeling.
Often a firm agrees to be taken over, but sometimes the takeover bid is hostile and unpopular.

3) Mergers and takeovers often lead to cost-cutting. This may mean making lots of people redundant, so they can lead to tension and uncertainty among workers.

See page 5 for more about franchising and how it works.

## Firms Can also Grow Through Franchising

1) Franchising is a good way of rapidly increasing both brand awareness and the market share of a firm's products without the usual costs and risks of opening a new outlet — the franchisee has to pay to start the franchise and takes on most of the risk.

2) By franchising, a firm can achieve greater economies of scale (see page 71) — they benefit from increased sales of their products. But franchises are run as separate businesses, which means the franchisor saves money on wages and other costs.

## Hitchcock takeover consultancy — Dial M for Merger...

Loads of new stuff to learn here — but I don't reckon any of it's too tricky. Just make sure you know the four main types of external expansion. Then scribble down a mini-essay on the advantages of each type. Don't forget franchising as well — you should know why a business might choose to grow using this method.

# Effects of Expansion on Stakeholders

Growing businesses have an impact on their stakeholders (see page 8) — and the effects aren't always good.

## The Growth of a Business Affects its Stakeholders

### Shareholders

Shareholders are likely to benefit from any increased profit that expansion brings. However, they might be asked to buy more shares and invest more money to help the business expand in the first place. Also, as a business grows and creates more shares, the power of smaller shareholders will be reduced. Sometimes these smaller shareholders join together to try to exert more influence.

### Employees

Employees should benefit from greater job security as larger businesses are less likely to fail than small firms. On the other hand large firms tend to be more hierarchical, so employees may feel less involved in the running of the business. As a result, workers in large firms are more likely to join a trade union in order to protect their interests than workers in small firms.

### Customers

Customers will benefit if the larger firm passes on any economies of scale in the form of lower prices. But the larger firm may have fewer competitors and so be able to charge higher prices. On their own, individual customers are often powerless to influence large businesses — but if a business upsets large numbers of its customers, it can be in trouble.

### Government

The government will collect more taxes as the business becomes larger and more profitable. However, some businesses can become so powerful and influential that it can be hard for governments to pass laws that threaten the interests of the business. The Government can investigate large firms if it thinks they are behaving in an anti-competitive way (i.e. if they're using their power to unfairly squeeze other firms out of the market).

### Local Community

Any negative impact the business causes locally, such as noise pollution or traffic congestion, is likely to be made worse as the business expands. On the other hand, it may make larger profits and so be able to invest in the community and create jobs. The local community may try to protect its interests by forming pressure groups to campaign against the business and try to persuade governments to pass laws limiting its negative impact.

### Suppliers

Suppliers should benefit from increased sales as a larger firm needs to buy more supplies. However, they will be in a weaker position when negotiating prices as more of their competitors will be keen to supply the large firm (and the large firm will be able to drive a hard bargain because of this).

## And I'm not talking about chubby vampire slayers...

All pretty straightforward here — when a business grows, it impacts on all the different stakeholders connected to that business. Make sure you know how each different set of stakeholders is affected by the growth of a business and how those stakeholders might react to protect their own interests.

# Business Ownership Structures

When a private limited company (page 4) has met certain minimum requirements (e.g. the number of <u>shareholders</u> and its record of <u>profitability</u>) it can choose to convert itself to a <u>public</u> limited company.

## Public Limited Companies Can Sell Shares to Anybody

1) Private limited companies can <u>only</u> sell new shares if <u>all</u> of the current shareholders <u>agree</u>.

2) A <u>public limited company</u> is formed when a private limited company is 'floated' on the <u>stock market</u>, allowing <u>any</u> member of the public to buy shares in the company.

3) This means that there is <u>much more</u> money available to the company in the form of share capital, which allows the firm to <u>expand</u> greatly.

See page 53 for more about issuing shares.

4) Many of the world's largest companies are public limited companies — British ones have <u>plc</u> at the end of the company name.

## There are Pros and Cons to Becoming a plc

Life <u>isn't</u> all beer and skittles for a plc — there are <u>downsides</u> too...

| Advantages | Disadvantages |
|---|---|
| 1) Still retain the main advantage of all limited companies — having <u>limited liability</u>. <br><br> 2) Can raise much more <u>capital</u> as a plc by <u>selling shares</u> through a <u>stock exchange</u> (since there are more potential buyers). <br><br> 3) Increased capital allows the company to <u>grow</u> and <u>diversify</u>. <br><br> 4) The <u>status</u> of the company is increased by becoming a plc, so <u>banks</u> are more willing to <u>lend money</u> to them. | 1) The shareholders <u>own</u> the company, but a <u>different</u> group of people (the directors) <u>control</u> the day-to-day running of the company. This is called '<u>divorce of ownership and control</u>' — the directors may make decisions that don't directly benefit the shareholders. This can lead to disagreements. <br><br> 2) There is always the threat that someone will buy enough shares to <u>take over</u> the company — if they can convince shareholders to sell. <br><br> 3) Shareholders generally want to make as much <u>profit</u> as possible, which can make it <u>difficult</u> for a plc to pursue other objectives, like helping the environment. |

She sells short - sleeved shirt shares by the sea shore.

## A Company's Objectives can Change as It Grows

1) <u>New</u> and <u>small businesses</u> are most likely to be concerned with <u>survival</u>.

2) As a business <u>grows</u>, its main objective will be to become, and stay, <u>profitable</u>.

3) Larger, established businesses will still aim to make a profit, but they often have the opportunity (and financial security) to also pursue <u>other objectives</u>, such as <u>dominating their market</u> or expanding <u>overseas</u>. But these other objectives will still aim to lead to more profit in the <u>long term</u>.

4) Over the last few years, many businesses have responded to pressure from consumers and have made <u>ethical</u> and <u>environmental issues</u> an important part of their objectives (see next page).

## Public limited — like the most exclusive parties...

Make sure you know how buying shares in a plc is different to buying them in a Ltd. You need to know the pros and cons of becoming a plc. This is a <u>favourite topic</u> for examiners — <u>learn</u> it but good, y'all.

# Social Influences

Businesses play a huge role in all our lives, and they can have both positive and negative effects on society. Many customers now prefer to buy from firms that have responsible and ethical policies.

## Businesses Have Social Costs and Social Benefits

Business activity can have costs and benefits that go beyond the buyer and seller. For example:

### Social Costs

1) Businesses can have environmental costs (i.e. they can damage the environment) — e.g. pollution from industry can lead to anything from a local nuisance to climate change.

2) Many resources used by businesses are non-renewable (e.g. coal and iron). If these run out, there's no way we can replace them.

3) Some businesses make products that can be harmful to people's health (e.g. tobacco and alcohol) — the government has to spend money to treat illnesses caused by these products.

4) Business activity can raise other ethical questions. For example, some people feel that certain businesses unfairly exploit cheap labour in developing countries, and that others carry out unnecessary animal testing.

### Social Benefits

1) Taxes on businesses' profits help pay for government services like schools and hospitals.

2) Businesses provide jobs for millions of people.

3) They provide all sorts of essential services to help keep the country moving (transport services, electricity, etc).

4) Goods provided by businesses can improve people's health (e.g. medicines), keep people safe (e.g. safer cars), or keep people happy (e.g. holidays).

Ethics are the moral principles of right or wrong.

## Social Issues can Affect Business Decisions

As consumers become more aware of ethical and social issues, many are changing their buying decisions — businesses are responding by changing their objectives to try to meet the demands of their customers.

1) Some firms now import their raw materials from fair-trade sources — this means they pay producers in developing countries higher prices so they can earn decent wages.

2) Some firms aim to carry out product development in an ethical way — e.g. using non-toxic materials, paying close attention to safety, and not using animal testing.

3) Many firms are changing their products and packaging to become more environmentally friendly. Products like electrical goods and cars are becoming much more energy efficient. Many businesses are reducing their carbon footprints by using less energy in their factories and offices.

4) Many businesses are trying to operate in a more sustainable way. They're using more renewable energy resources (such as wind and solar power), and recycling more of their materials.

## It's In a Firm's Interests to Take These Issues Seriously

1) Taking ethical and environmental issues seriously can give firms a competitive advantage — a 'green' or 'socially responsible' image can attract new customers and increase sales. The main disadvantage is cost. Using fair-trade materials is usually more expensive and the costs of cleaning up pollution can be high.

2) Pressure groups such as Greenpeace and Friends of the Earth campaign to raise awareness of environmental issues. They target the businesses they believe are causing most damage to the environment. The reputation and brand image of a business can be harmed by pressure groups — this may lead to lower profits.

## No animals were harmed in the making of this page...

...but several writers were prodded with forks. Not really — CGP is an ethical and socially responsible business. Ethical policies can increase costs, but there's also plenty of demand for ethical goods.

# Multinational Firms

Sometimes a firm decides to <u>expand overseas</u>, so it has operations in <u>more than one country</u>.
These firms are called <u>multinational enterprises</u> (MNEs) or <u>transnational corporations</u> (TNCs).

## Firms Become Multinational for Many Reasons

The main factors influencing the location of a business are on page 10. They basically boil down to two
things: keeping <u>costs</u> to a <u>minimum</u>, and <u>maximising revenue</u>. Many businesses think that the <u>best
compromise</u> between these two things is to locate <u>overseas</u>. Some of the reasons why firms do this include:

1) By producing in various countries they can keep <u>transport costs</u> to a minimum.

2) They can increase their knowledge of <u>local market conditions</u>.

3) They can avoid <u>trade barriers</u> by producing <u>inside a country</u>.

4) They can reduce risks from <u>foreign exchange</u> fluctuations.

5) They can gain access to <u>raw materials</u> or <u>cheap labour</u>.

6) By employing <u>expert accountants</u> and shuffling money <u>between countries</u>,
   big companies can <u>avoid paying tax</u>.

7) They can win <u>subsidies</u> from governments and force workers to accept
   <u>lower wages</u> by <u>threatening to relocate</u> production in another country.

We'll employ Filipino labour, sell in America, and pay tax in the Cayman Islands.

## MNEs Can Benefit the Host Country...

1) MNEs are often a source of <u>foreign investment</u>. And they <u>create employment</u> for locals.

2) MNEs bring their own methods of working, giving the host country access to <u>foreign technology</u>
   and working methods — like with Japanese car producers in the UK.

3) The <u>profits</u> of the MNE can be a source of <u>taxation revenue</u> for the host country's government
   — <u>in theory</u> at least (see point 2 below).

4) The MNE will probably <u>export</u> goods from the host country to foreign markets. The revenue from these
   export sales may improve the host country's <u>balance of payments</u> (this is the difference between the
   money coming into a country from sales of <u>exports</u>, and money being spent by the country on <u>imports</u>).

## ...But They Can Cause Plenty of Problems Too

1) The jobs created by MNEs are often <u>unskilled</u>. Workers often work for <u>long hours</u>,
   with <u>lower wages</u> than they'd get in the MNE's home country. Some people argue
   that these workers are treated <u>unfairly</u> by the MNE.

2) In return for locating in their country, the MNEs may ask for <u>reduced tax rates</u> and even <u>subsidies</u>
   from the government — or ask the government to build <u>roads</u> and airport links. It could <u>cost
   governments money</u> to host an MNE if taxation revenue is less than they expected.

3) The MNE, benefiting from economies of scale, might drive out <u>local industries</u>.

4) They can exert a <u>strong influence</u> on the government to <u>change laws</u> that increase their costs.
   E.g. they might lobby for a reduction in <u>environmental controls</u> or <u>worker protection</u> laws.

5) MNEs can cause <u>environmental degradation</u> in developing countries that lasts for a long time.
   The company's owners probably <u>don't live there</u>, so they don't see the impact of the damage.

6) When MNEs locate in poorer countries, the benefits to the country are often <u>much less than</u> the
   benefits to MNE <u>shareholders</u> — after all, the point of locating there is to <u>maximise profits</u>.

## But that's enough about MNE — let's talk about you...

You have to <u>make up your own mind</u> whether MNEs are good or bad — in an exam, there's no right or
wrong answer, it's <u>how you argue it</u> that counts. Learn everything on this page, then <u>think about it</u> and
scribble an answer to the mini-essay question: "Are MNEs <u>good, bad, or a bit of both</u>?"

# Revision Summary for Section Six

Well, there you are, the first section on the big boys of business is finished. And the way to make sure you've learned it is to check you know the answers to these questions. Note down any questions you find tricky and then go over the stuff again until you can do them easily. I know it's a pain but trust me, it's the only way...

1) Explain five reasons why firms choose to expand.

2) Give one benefit and one problem of internal expansion.

3) What's the difference between internal and external expansion?

4) Explain three methods of external expansion a firm can use.

5) Smellsbad Rhubarb Chutney Ltd., a well known rhubarb chutney manufacturer, merges with the following firms. Which type of firm is Smellsbad Rhubarb Chutney Ltd. merging with in each case?
   - a) Quality Rhubarb Chutneys Manufacturers Ltd.
   - b) Exotic Chutney Shops Ltd.
   - c) Megalarge Knickers Producers Ltd.
   - d) Rhubarb Farms Ltd.

6) Explain why takeovers and mergers are not always successful.

7) Explain the benefits to a business of growing through franchising.

8) Describe how the following groups are likely to be affected by a firm's growth:
   - a) the firm's employees,
   - b) the firm's shareholders,
   - c) the firm's customers,
   - d) the firm's suppliers,
   - e) the government,
   - f) the local community.

9) How might each of the above groups try to protect their interests as the firm grows?

10) How do private and public limited companies differ in the way that their shares can be sold?

11) Describe two advantages to a private limited company of becoming a plc.

12) Explain what is meant by the 'divorce of ownership and control'.
Give two other disadvantages of becoming a plc.

13) Explain how a company's objectives will typically change as it grows.

14) Describe two social costs and two social benefits of business activity.

15) Give four examples of how some businesses are acting in a more socially responsible way.

16) Describe one cost and one benefit to a business of developing a 'green image'.

17) How can environmental pressure groups affect businesses?

18) Explain three advantages of operating as an MNE.

19) Give two benefits and two problems for a country of hosting an MNE.

20) Are you ready for Section Seven?

# Product — The Product Life Cycle

It's back to the four Ps of the marketing mix (see p.12) and it's time to look at the product again. Even firms that come up with great products will find that they don't sell well forever — all products have a life cycle.

## Demand for a Product Changes Over Time

All products go through the same life cycle — but the sales life of some products is longer than others'. For example, the sales life of most cars is about ten years, but the sales life of many computer games is only a few months. Whatever the product, its marketing mix will need to change during its life cycle.

1) **DEVELOPMENT** is the first stage of a product's life cycle. Research and Development (R&D) and market research are used to develop an idea and turn it into a marketable product.
   - Scientific research is often vital for product development. A lot of scientific research is done in universities. It's often "pure" science — without any kind of commercial aim.
   - Large businesses often then have teams of "applied" scientists, who try to use recent scientific discoveries to develop new or improved products to sell.
   - One aim during product development is to find the most cost-effective materials and methods to use.

2) **INTRODUCTION** comes next — the product is launched and put on sale for the first time. This is usually backed up with lots of advertising and sales promotions. Place is also an important P here — there's no point launching a product in places where nobody will be interested in buying it.

3) **GROWTH** During this phase, sales and profitability increase, until the product becomes established.

4) **MATURITY** Sales are at their peak. Promotion becomes less important at this stage — businesses will continue to advertise the product, but less than at its launch. As the product's popularity grows, businesses will try to make the product more widely available.
   Towards the end of this phase, the market becomes saturated and there's no more room to expand.

5) **DECLINE** Eventually sales start to fall as rival products take over, and the product becomes obsolete.

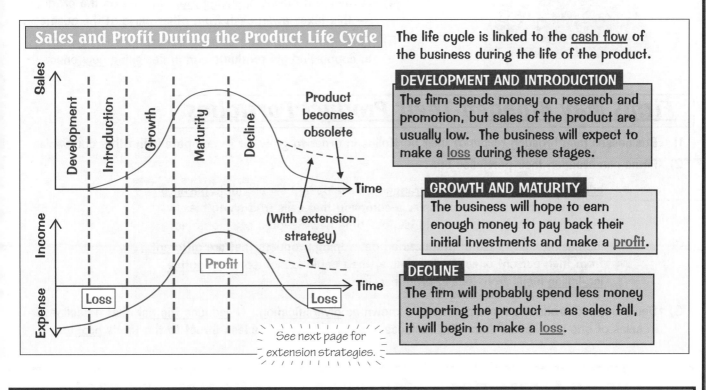

**Sales and Profit During the Product Life Cycle**

The life cycle is linked to the cash flow of the business during the life of the product.

**DEVELOPMENT AND INTRODUCTION**
The firm spends money on research and promotion, but sales of the product are usually low. The business will expect to make a loss during these stages.

**GROWTH AND MATURITY**
The business will hope to earn enough money to pay back their initial investments and make a profit.

**DECLINE**
The firm will probably spend less money supporting the product — as sales fall, it will begin to make a loss.

See next page for extension strategies.

## Marketing a product? Sounds more like parenting...

So, make a product that people want. Love it and nurture it throughout its life cycle. Then watch as it gets old, becomes unpopular and starts losing you money — products can be so ungrateful. Try not to cry.

# Product — Product Portfolios

So, you set up a fantastic business. You had a great <u>product</u>. It sold really well. And then not so well. And then not well at all. Finally, you accepted that your lovely product was in <u>decline</u>. You worried for your firm. What to do... And then it came to you... <u>New</u> products... <u>More</u> products... A whole <u>portfolio</u> of products...

## Businesses Need a Variety of Products

1) A <u>product portfolio</u> is the <u>range</u> of <u>different products</u> that a firm sells.

2) Most large businesses will have products at <u>different stages</u> of the product life-cycle, giving them a <u>balanced portfolio</u>.

3) They'll have some products that have reached the <u>peak</u> of their sales — bringing in <u>lots of money</u> with little investment. These are responsible for most of the business's income.

4) However, at some point these products will start to <u>decline</u> and will have to be <u>replaced</u>. So the firm needs to have products in the <u>development</u> and <u>introduction</u> stages that will later grow to <u>maturity</u> and take their place. These products still need <u>lots of investment</u>.

> I don't mean to be rude mate, but you look like you need an awful lot of investment...

## Firms May Try to Extend the Life of Products in Decline

1) Although the sales of all products will eventually decline, firms can take action to <u>extend their life</u>.

> Scalpel... sutures... sale sign. Come on people, let's move — there's a life to extend here.

2) They might decide to use an <u>extension strategy</u> during the decline phase of the life cycle — e.g. making changes to the <u>design</u> or offering discounts on the <u>price</u>.

3) If the extension strategy works, the product will make profit for <u>longer</u>.

4) However, it means <u>spending more</u> money on the product — this <u>takes away</u> cash from other parts of the business.

5) Firms have to strike a <u>balance</u> between investing money in supporting <u>old</u> products and in designing <u>new</u> ones.

## Firms May Broaden Their Product Portfolios

1) Businesses may <u>broaden</u> (expand) their portfolios in order to grow, or to compete with other companies.

2) Firms can broaden their portfolios by...

- <u>adding</u> products to an <u>existing range</u> by developing new products <u>based on</u> their current ones. For example, a company that sells fruit smoothies made from local produce could launch some new flavours of smoothies.

- increasing their range of products by developing products that are <u>different</u> from their current ones. For example, they could launch some <u>smoothie ice-lollies</u> made from locally-produced fruit.

3) Designing and producing more products is known as <u>diversification</u>. It <u>reduces the risk</u> that a decline in sales of one product will harm the business, meaning that there's less threat to the firm's <u>profits</u>.

## Extension Strategies — for when your homework's late...

So, a <u>portfolio</u> is a firm's <u>range</u> of products. Like many things in life (e.g. diet, mental state) it should be <u>balanced</u>. Like others (e.g. minds, horizons) it might need to be <u>broadened</u>. Simple. Oh, and firms may try to <u>extend the life</u> of products. Instead of letting them retire gracefully. Some people have no respect...

# Price — Pricing Strategies

On to the second of the four Ps — <u>price</u>. "Huzzah", I hear you cry. Getting pricing <u>right</u> is mega important if a firm is to be successful, so firms develop <u>pricing strategies</u>. There are <u>two main types</u>...

## ① Market-Led Pricing

A firm will use a <u>market-led</u> pricing strategy if the <u>price</u> of the product helps consumers decide whether to buy it — which is <u>most of the time</u>. There are four different pricing methods you need to know.

1) `PENETRATION PRICING` is where a firm charges a very <u>low</u> price when the product is <u>new</u> to get lots of people <u>interested</u> in it.

2) `LOSS LEADER PRICING` is when a price is set <u>below cost</u> (this is a kind of penetration pricing really). Once the product has become <u>established</u> the firm will <u>increase</u> the price. This happens with new consumer products where existing products have <u>brand loyalty</u> — magazines are a good example.

3) `PRICE SKIMMING` is the <u>opposite</u> of penetration pricing. Firms charge a <u>high price</u> to begin with — this helps make the product <u>desirable</u> to people with large incomes. When the product has become established the firm will <u>lower the price</u> to help it become a <u>mass-market</u> product. This happens a lot with consumer goods based on <u>new technology</u>, such as plasma-screen TVs.

It may sound steep, but this is cutting-edge technology.

4) `COMPETITIVE PRICING` This is where the firm has to charge <u>similar</u> prices to <u>other firms</u>. It happens most when there is lots of choice and not much product differentiation — e.g. petrol.

## ② Cost-Plus Pricing

Firms will use this method if they are <u>not</u> in <u>price competition</u> with other producers — though of course they can still only charge what people are prepared to pay. There are <u>two main ways</u> it can be worked out — using a <u>mark-up</u> and using a <u>profit margin</u>. See page 56 for more on profit margins.

### EXAMPLE

1) **USING A MARK-UP**

Work out how much the product costs and then add a <u>percentage mark-up</u>. So if the product <u>costs £2</u> to make, and you want a <u>25% mark-up</u>, you'd sell it for £2 + 25% = <u>£2.50</u>.

Using a 10 000% mark-up, I'll have all the money in the world by, ooh, Tuesday. I'm the best entrepreneur ever.

2) **USING A PROFIT MARGIN**

Work out how much the product costs and increase by the required <u>profit margin</u>. So if the product <u>costs £2</u> to make, and you want a <u>20% profit margin</u>, this means that £2 is 80% of your required selling price.
So 80% = 200p
1% = 200 ÷ 80 = 2.5p
100% = 2.5p × 100 = 250p
So you'd sell it for <u>£2.50</u>.

Careful here — notice that a <u>25% mark-up</u> is the <u>same</u> as a <u>20% profit margin</u>. That's because the <u>mark-up</u> is expressed as a percentage of the <u>cost of making</u> the product — 50p is 25% of £2.

But the <u>profit margin</u> is expressed as a percentage of the <u>selling price</u> — 50p is 20% of £2.50.

## You can't put a price on happiness...

...but you can make <u>examiners</u> happy by knowing about <u>prices</u>. And if they're happy, <u>you're happy</u>. So if you want to be happy, learn about <u>market-led</u> pricing and <u>cost-plus</u> pricing. It's cheaper than therapy.

# Promotion

Here's P number three — <u>promotion</u>. Don't make the mistake of thinking promotion is <u>just about advertising</u> — nothing as dull and easy as that. Here are various other ways the firm can remind you that they exist. Enjoy.

## Sales Promotion — *You Need to Know Seven Methods*

1)  <u>Discounts</u>. Stamping '10% off' on the label is likely to get a product noticed.
2)  <u>Product trials</u>. Invite people to taste new Smello Baked Beans for free.
3)  <u>Free gifts</u>. Buy a skateboard and get a free MP3 Player with built-in toaster.
4)  <u>Buy One Get One Free</u> (BOGOF). Or buy one get something else free.
5)  <u>Competitions</u>. Say why new Smello Baked Beans are good for you in less than twenty words — and win a year's supply free.
6)  <u>Point-of-sale advertising</u>. Put tins of new Smello Baked Beans in a special display case at the front of the supermarket.
7)  <u>Use of credit</u>. A good way to get someone to buy a product is to let them buy now but pay later — through hire purchase or a store charge card.

These are also called <u>point-of-sale</u> promotions — because that's where they happen.

### Direct Marketing Goes Straight to the Customer

1)  In <u>direct marketing</u>, the business contacts the potential customer <u>directly</u> without going through other media. E.g. Saucy Co. might mail out vouchers for 10p off a bottle of their new Awfully Hot Sauce.
2)  The customer is invited to make a <u>direct response</u> to the message — they might want to use their voucher next time they're at the supermarket.
3)  An important benefit of direct marketing is that a business can <u>measure</u> its <u>success</u>. If they send out 20,000 vouchers and 4952 people use them at the shops, the promotion has had a success rate of nearly 25%.
4)  The problem is that it creates <u>junk mail</u> and <u>spam e-mail</u>. Some people <u>can't stand</u> businesses that send out junk — but there's <u>no way</u> for a business to measure how many people they've <u>annoyed</u>.

### Businesses Can Sponsor Organisations and Events

Businesses sometimes help to pay for events such as sports tournaments, TV shows and exhibitions. In return, it can <u>display its name</u> at the event. This is called <u>sponsorship</u>, and examples are everywhere:

1)  **SPORT** A large business might stamp its brand name all over an international competition. A smaller business will have to make do with the local Sunday League team, but the aim is the same.
2)  **TELEVISION** Some soap operas and weather reports are sponsored by well-known brands.
3)  **THE ARTS** Theatres, art galleries and concert halls are often short of cash — businesses can step in to sponsor them. It makes the business look <u>classy</u> — but some people think art and business <u>don't mix</u>.

Sponsorship can create a <u>high profile</u> for your business or brand name. But if the thing you're sponsoring starts to get <u>bad publicity</u>, your company's image suffers too.

You need to know about advertising as well — see page 17 for this.

### And now a word from our sponsor...

Businesses want you to <u>know about their products</u> — even if you live in a cave with no electricity. They'll tempt you with offers at the <u>shops</u>. They'll bombard you with coupons through the <u>post</u>. They'll <u>sponsor</u> your local chess team. This page was brought to you by CGP — books for <u>gorgeous</u> people.

# Place — Where the Product is Sold

Place is the fourth and final P. Celebrations all round... Well, not quite yet — you need to learn about channels of distribution first. Put simply, these are how products get from manufacturers to consumers.

## Distribution Channels Can be Direct or Indirect

There are four distribution channels that you need to know about —
1, 2 and 3 are indirect channels, 4 is a direct channel.

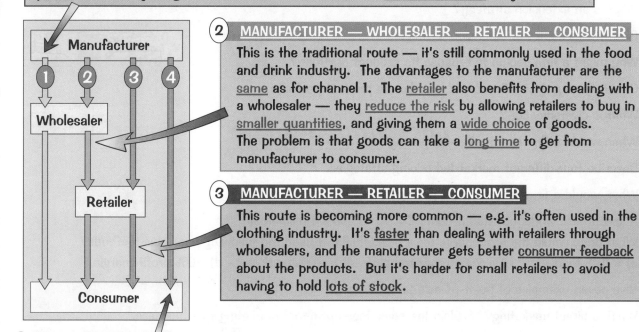

**1  MANUFACTURER — WHOLESALER — CONSUMER**

Here, consumers buy the product from a cash and carry warehouse. It's good for the manufacturer because they get bulk orders and the wholesaler takes on the cost of storing the products and the risk of not selling them. The consumer often pays lower prices than if they bought from a retailer — but levels of customer service may be lower.

**2  MANUFACTURER — WHOLESALER — RETAILER — CONSUMER**

This is the traditional route — it's still commonly used in the food and drink industry. The advantages to the manufacturer are the same as for channel 1. The retailer also benefits from dealing with a wholesaler — they reduce the risk by allowing retailers to buy in smaller quantities, and giving them a wide choice of goods. The problem is that goods can take a long time to get from manufacturer to consumer.

**3  MANUFACTURER — RETAILER — CONSUMER**

This route is becoming more common — e.g. it's often used in the clothing industry. It's faster than dealing with retailers through wholesalers, and the manufacturer gets better consumer feedback about the products. But it's harder for small retailers to avoid having to hold lots of stock.

**4  MANUFACTURER — CONSUMER**

This is now very popular — examples include factory shops, mail order, telesales and internet selling. It's the fastest channel, and often cheapest for the consumer. But it can be more difficult for consumers to shop around (manufacturers usually only sell their own products, but a retailer would probably stock goods from a range of manufacturers), and customer service levels may not be as good.

### A Typical Exam Scenario — Selling Frozen Food

New Twists Ltd. are a small frozen food manufacturer. They make microwaveable meals, based on traditional recipes, but with a new twist. They are trying to decide the most appropriate distribution channel for their new product of Real Ratatouille (with real rat). Explain what you would recommend to New Twists Ltd.

*'Selling frozen food directly to consumers will be difficult, because you cannot post frozen food — it needs to be delivered quickly. New Twists should probably try to sell to wholesalers (or perhaps big supermarket chains), as this will reduce their delivery costs but still allow their products to reach a wide range of consumers.'*

Hmmph...

## Channel 4 news — it gets straight to the point (of sale)...

Make sure you learn the four distribution channels — cover the diagram and see if you can draw it.
Try writing a mini-essay on the pros and cons of each method. Reward yourself with a banana or something.

# Revision Summary for Section Seven

Here we go again — a lovely revision summary to check that you can still remember all that interesting stuff on marketing that you've just learned. I knew you'd be pleased. When you've finished the questions (not before, mind) and you want to check your profit-margin and mark-up answers, you'll find them in a box at the bottom. No peeking though, otherwise I'll slap your legs.

1) Describe the five stages of the product life cycle.

2) When are a product's sales highest?
a) development;   b) maturity;   c) January.

3) Describe how the amount of advertising might change throughout the life cycle of a product.

4) What is a product portfolio?

5) What is an extension strategy?

6) Give two examples of extension strategies.

7) Why might a firm decide to broaden its product portfolio?

8) Give two ways that a firm could broaden its product portfolio.

9) What is diversification?

10) When would a firm use market-led pricing?

11) Describe four different market-led pricing strategies.

12) When would a firm use cost-plus pricing?

13) A sports firm works out that it costs £4.50 to make a basketball.
What price would the firm charge for a basketball if it used the following cost-plus methods?
a) a 15% mark-up;   b) a 20% profit-margin;   c) a 30% mark-up;   d) 40% profit-margin.

14) Give seven examples of point-of-sale promotions.

15) What is direct marketing? Explain the advantages of direct marketing to a business.

16) What is sponsorship?

17) Give three examples of things that firms might sponsor.

18) Give a disadvantage of sponsorship.

19) Describe three indirect channels of distribution.

20) Describe what's meant by 'direct channel of distribution'.

21) Why might consumers find it an advantage to buy from a wholesaler rather than a retailer?

22) Why might manufacturers like dealing with a wholesaler?

23) What are the advantages and disadvantages of a direct distribution channel?

13. a) £5.18;  b) £5.63;
c) £5.85;  d) £7.50.

# Sources of Finance — Large Firms

Larger firms find it <u>easier</u> to raise finance than smaller firms. Being bigger and <u>more established</u> means they are <u>less</u> likely to go bust — so they are less of a <u>credit risk</u> to banks.

## Established Firms Can Get Finance from Various Sources

You saw the main sources of finance available to small businesses on page 20. As firms <u>grow</u> and become more established, <u>new</u> sources of finance become available to them:

Looks like a classic case of profit retention I'm afraid

1) **RETAINED PROFITS** are profits that the owners have decided to <u>plough back</u> into the business <u>after</u> they've paid themselves a <u>dividend</u>. But larger companies (e.g. plcs) are under <u>pressure</u> from shareholders to give <u>large dividends</u>, reducing the amount of profit they can retain.

2) **RE-INVESTED SAVINGS** Large, successful firms may have used retained profit from previous years to build up <u>bank savings</u> or buy <u>stocks and shares</u>. They can use these to get cash quickly if they need it (but as my ol' mum used to say — once it's gone, it's <u>gone</u>).

3) **FIXED ASSETS** Firms can raise cash by <u>selling</u> fixed assets (e.g. machinery or buildings) that are <u>no longer in use</u>. There is a <u>limit</u> to how many assets you can sell though — sell too many and you can't go on trading.

*Firms sometimes use 'sale and lease back' — they rent the asset back after selling it (often done with land and buildings).*

4) **SHARES** A limited company can <u>issue more shares</u>. The money raised does not have to be repaid to shareholders — but more shares means <u>less control</u> for the <u>existing owners</u>.

5) **DEBENTURES** Limited companies can issue <u>debentures</u> to the public. These are <u>long-term loans</u> which the firm commits itself to <u>repay with interest</u> — for up to <u>25 years</u> or so. People who are issued with debentures <u>don't own</u> any part of the business — they only <u>lend</u> the business money.

6) **LOANS/MORTGAGES** Larger businesses may still need to use bank loans or mortgages, which have to be <u>repaid with interest</u>. But it's much <u>easier</u> for large firms to get loans — banks are more willing to lend them money as there's <u>less risk</u> of them <u>failing</u>. Also, they have <u>more assets</u> to use as <u>collateral</u> (p.20).

## Different Situations Need Different Sources of Finance

Several factors <u>influence</u> which sources are <u>available</u> to a particular business, and which it should <u>actually use</u>:

1) <u>Type of company</u> — not all companies have access to <u>all types</u> of finance:
   - Some types of business may <u>not have</u> fixed assets available to sell.
   - Only <u>limited companies</u> can issue shares and debentures.

2) <u>Amount of money needed</u> — a company wouldn't issue more shares to buy a toaster. <u>Small amounts</u> of money usually come from <u>retained profits</u> or <u>savings</u>. <u>Larger</u> amounts of money, (e.g. for new property or machinery) are more likely to need a <u>loan</u> or <u>mortgage</u>.

3) <u>Length of time</u> the finance is needed for — it'd be daft to take out a mortgage because a customer is a week late paying an invoice. Using <u>savings</u> or an arranged <u>overdraft</u> from a bank should be able to see a business through a <u>short-term</u> lack of finance.

4) <u>Cost of the finance</u> — some sources, e.g. bank loans and overdrafts, are <u>more expensive</u> than others as the money has to be paid back <u>with interest</u>.

5) <u>State of the economy</u> — if interest rates are <u>high</u>, people are more <u>reluctant to invest</u> in businesses because of the risks involved, and will put their money in secure bank and building society accounts instead. Also, when interest rates are high, loans and mortgages become <u>more expensive</u> for the business to take out.

100% PURE Money Sauce

## Debentures — a long-term loan of false teeth...

Examiners love to test whether you can <u>identify</u> the right source of finance to meet the <u>needs</u> of a business. You need to know the <u>different</u> sources of finance and the <u>factors</u> that affect which source a firm will choose.

# The Trading, Profit and Loss Account

The trading, profit and loss account records the difference between the firm's <u>income</u> and the <u>cost</u> of running the business over a period of <u>one year</u>. It contains <u>three sections</u>.

## ① The Trading Account

1) This section is coloured <u>yellow</u> in the example.
   It records the firm's <u>gross</u> profit or loss (see below).

2) <u>Turnover</u> is another word for <u>revenue</u> — it records the value of all <u>products sold</u> during the year.
   <u>Cost of sales</u> records how much it cost to <u>make the products</u> that were sold during the year — the <u>direct costs</u>.

3) There has to be an <u>adjustment for stock</u>. Say at the start of the year Yummo Chocolates had <u>200 tons</u> of cocoa in stock, then during the year they <u>bought in</u> 2000 tons, and at the end of the year they had <u>150 tons left</u>. That means they <u>used and sold</u> 2050 tons of cocoa — <u>this figure</u> is used to work out the cost of sales.

4) <u>Gross profit</u> is the <u>difference</u> between the <u>revenue from selling</u> the chocolate and the <u>direct costs</u> of <u>making</u> it. This means:

   gross profit = revenue – direct costs

*Numbers in brackets are <u>negative</u>.*

**Trading, Profit and Loss Account**
**Yummo Chocolates Ltd.**
**Year ending 31st March 2009**

|  | £000 | £000 |
|---|---|---|
| Turnover............................ |  | 180 |
| Cost of sales: |  |  |
|    Opening stock......... | 3 |  |
|    Purchases.............. | 15 |  |
|  | 18 |  |
| Minus closing stock......... | (5) |  |
| Cost of sales = .................. |  | (13) |
| Gross profit =...................... |  | 167 |
| **Minus expenses** |  |  |
|    Wages and salaries.. | 93 |  |
|    Rent and rates........ | 10 |  |
|    Office expenses...... | 28 |  |
|    Advertising............. | 5 |  |
|    Depreciation........... | 8 |  |
|    Other expenses....... | 3 |  |
| Expenses = ........................ |  | (147) |
| Operating profit = ............... |  | 20 |
| Interest payable .................. |  | (2) |
| Profit before tax (Net profit)... |  | 18 |
| Taxation ............................. |  | (3) |
| Dividends ........................... |  | (9) |
| Retained profit ................... |  | 6 |

## ② The Profit and Loss Account

1) This section is coloured <u>blue</u> — it records all the <u>indirect costs</u> of running the business. It does <u>not</u> include the costs of <u>buying</u> <u>assets</u> such as machinery for the <u>first time</u> — but it does include the costs of <u>using</u> them and <u>replacing</u> them (see point 2 below).

2) Some assets <u>wear out</u> with use — eventually they need replacing. Firms usually <u>set aside</u> money each year so that there will be money to <u>buy replacements</u> when they're needed. This is treated as a business expense — it's called <u>depreciation</u>.

3) The money left after paying all the costs of running the business is called <u>operating profit</u>.

4) Finally, any <u>interest</u> paid or received is included. What is left is true profit — <u>net profit</u>.

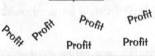

Profit Profit Profit Profit Profit Profit Profit Profit

There are <u>two methods</u> of calculating depreciation.

1) <u>Straight line method</u>. This is the <u>easy</u> way. If a machine costs <u>£5000</u> and will wear out after about <u>5 years</u>, the depreciation is simply <u>£1000</u> each year.

2) <u>Reducing balance method</u>. This depreciates the machinery by a <u>percentage of its value</u> each year — a <u>£5000</u> machine might depreciate by <u>25%</u> each year.

- Depreciation in year 1 = 25% of £5000 = <u>£1250</u>. The value is now £5000 – £1250 = £3750.
- Depreciation in year 2 = 25% of £3750 = <u>£938</u>. The value is now £3750 – £938 = £2812. And so on.

## ③ The Appropriation Account

1) Coloured <u>mauve</u> on the example. This is only included for <u>limited company</u> accounts.

2) It records <u>where</u> the profit has gone — to the <u>government</u> as tax, to <u>shareholders</u> as dividends, or kept in the business as <u>retained profit</u>.

## Net profit — Wimbledon are selling off old stock...

Some of this is a bit tricky, so take your time and make sure you know <u>what</u> is included in each part of the accounts and <u>why</u>. Memorise and copy out the <u>headings</u> — then <u>explain</u> what each one means. Grand.

# The Trading, Profit and Loss Account

Yep, you guessed it — another page all about profit and loss accounts. You need to know how you can use profit and loss accounts to see how a business is performing, and who might be interested in this information.

## Profit and Loss Accounts Show Business Performance...

The profit and loss account can be used to assess how well a business has performed in that year.
The profit and loss accounts from two consecutive years for a yacht-building firm are shown below:

In 2007-08, Boats Ahoy Ltd. performed well.

**Trading, Profit and Loss Account**
**Boats Ahoy Ltd.**
**Year ending 31st March 2008**

| | £m | £m |
|---|---|---|
| Turnover | | 870 |
| Cost of sales: | | |
| Opening stock | 89 | |
| Purchases | 420 | |
| | 509 | |
| Minus closing stock | (75) | |
| Cost of sales = | | (434) |
| Gross profit = | | 436 |
| | | |
| Minus expenses | | |
| Wages and salaries | 92 | |
| Rent and rates | 75 | |
| Office expenses | 35 | |
| Advertising | 5 | |
| Depreciation | 35 | |
| Other expenses | 68 | |
| Expenses = | | (310) |
| Operating profit = | | 126 |
| | | |
| Interest payable | | (20) |
| Profit before tax (Net profit)... | | 106 |
| | | |
| Taxation | | (15.9) |
| Dividends | | (18) |
| Retained profit | | 72.1 |

They made a profit of £106m...

...and had retained profits of £72.1m.

In 2008-09 they did not perform as well.

There was a high level of stock left at the end of the year — showing a poor response to low sales. Production should have been reduced as demand fell.

**Trading, Profit and Loss Account**
**Boats Ahoy Ltd.**
**Year ending 31st March 2009**

| | £m | £m |
|---|---|---|
| Turnover | | 805 |
| Cost of sales: | | |
| Opening stock | 75 | |
| Purchases | 430 | |
| | 505 | |
| Minus closing stock | (90) | |
| Cost of sales = | | (415) |
| Gross profit = | | 390 |
| | | |
| Minus expenses | | |
| Wages and salaries | 125 | |
| Rent and rates | 80 | |
| Office expenses | 55 | |
| Advertising | 10 | |
| Depreciation | 35 | |
| Other expenses | 75 | |
| Expenses = | | (380) |
| Operating profit = | | 10 |
| | | |
| Interest payable | | (20) |
| Profit before tax (Net profit)... | | -10 |
| | | |
| Taxation | | (0) |
| Dividends | | (18) |
| Retained profit | | -28 |

They made a loss of £10m...

...and yet still gave out dividends of £18m. The share dividend (see below) should be linked to how successful the company has been.

Taxation is zero because the firm made no profit.

Sales revenue fell by £65m. This is a percentage change of −7.5% from 2008:

% change =
(805 − 870) ÷ 870
= −0.075 = −7.5%

Wages increased by £33m. Expenses increased by £70m overall.

The directors have allowed costs to increase at a time when income is falling. This suggests poor management.

## ...Which is Useful Information for a Firm's Stakeholders

Profit and loss accounts are useful to people who have an interest in the firm's performance — i.e. the firm's stakeholders (see page 8). Some stakeholders who might use the profit and loss account include:

1) Existing shareholders are usually entitled to a share of the profits (called the share dividend). Potential shareholders will look at how much profit the business makes to help them decide if the business is worth investing in. Shareholders may also use the profit and loss account to assess the performance of the directors who are responsible for running the business.

2) Employees will want to know if the business is making a profit or loss — a profitable business could afford to give them a pay rise, but a loss-making business might make some workers redundant.

3) The government receives corporation tax from the business. The profit and loss account is used to calculate how much tax the business needs to pay.

## Business performance — it ain't no song and dance...

I reckon this page makes it a little bit easier to see how a profit and loss account can show how a business is doing. Cover the page and scribble down all the people who might be interested in this information.

# Profitability Ratios

I know what you're thinking... those <u>profit and loss accounts</u> are kinda <u>tricky</u>. I mean... there are numbers, numbers everywhere. Profitability ratios are a way to try to make <u>sense</u> of them.
Like all ratios, they involve <u>dividing</u> one number by another number.

## Gross Profit Margin <u>Ignores Indirect Costs</u>

Profit margins basically show you what <u>happens</u> to <u>each pound</u> spent by a customer.
There are two types — the first of these is <u>gross profit margin</u>...

**GROSS PROFIT MARGIN** — this is the fraction of <u>every pound</u> spent by customers that <u>doesn't</u> go <u>directly</u> towards making a product.

> Gross profit margin = gross profit ÷ sales (turnover)

For 2009, Yummo Chocolates' <u>trading, profit and loss account</u> shows its gross profit was <u>£167,000</u> and their <u>turnover</u> was <u>£180,000</u>.
This means the gross profit margin was:

$$167,000 ÷ 180,000 = \underline{0.9278}, \text{ or } \underline{92.78\%}.$$

Or, if you prefer, you can think of it like this...

*This is part of the trading account from p54.*

| | |
|---|---|
| Turnover.............................. | 180 |
| Cost of sales: | |
|    Opening stock......... | 3 |
|    Purchases.............. | 15 |
| | 18 |
| Minus closing stock.........| (5) |
| Cost of sales = ................. | (13) |
| Gross profit =...................... | 167 |

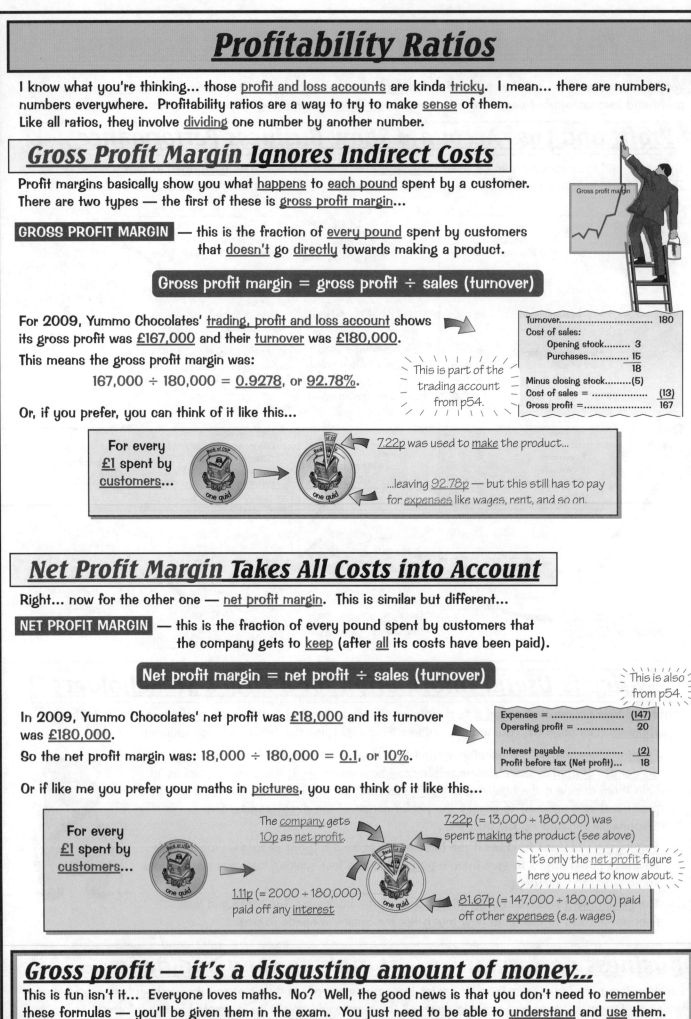

For every £1 spent by <u>customers</u>...

7.22p was used to <u>make</u> the product...

...leaving <u>92.78p</u> — but this still has to pay for <u>expenses</u> like wages, rent, and so on.

## Net Profit Margin <u>Takes All Costs into Account</u>

Right... now for the other one — <u>net profit margin</u>. This is similar but different...

**NET PROFIT MARGIN** — this is the fraction of every pound spent by customers that the company gets to <u>keep</u> (after <u>all</u> its costs have been paid).

> Net profit margin = net profit ÷ sales (turnover)

*This is also from p54.*

In 2009, Yummo Chocolates' net profit was <u>£18,000</u> and its turnover was <u>£180,000</u>.

So the net profit margin was: $18,000 ÷ 180,000 = \underline{0.1}, \text{ or } \underline{10\%}$.

| | |
|---|---|
| Expenses = ...................... | (147) |
| Operating profit = .............. | 20 |
| Interest payable .................. | (2) |
| Profit before tax (Net profit)... | 18 |

Or if like me you prefer your maths in <u>pictures</u>, you can think of it like this...

For every £1 spent by <u>customers</u>...

The <u>company</u> gets 10p as <u>net profit</u>.

<u>7.22p</u> (= 13,000 ÷ 180,000) was spent <u>making</u> the product (see above)

*It's only the <u>net profit</u> figure here you need to know about.*

<u>1.11p</u> (= 2000 ÷ 180,000) paid off any <u>interest</u>

<u>81.67p</u> (= 147,000 ÷ 180,000) paid off other <u>expenses</u> (e.g. wages)

## Gross profit — it's a disgusting amount of money...

This is fun isn't it... Everyone loves maths. No? Well, the good news is that you don't need to <u>remember</u> these formulas — you'll be given them in the exam. You just need to be able to <u>understand</u> and <u>use</u> them.

# The Balance Sheet — Net Assets

The balance sheet is quite <u>tricky</u> — but the <u>basic idea</u> is pretty simple. It records where the business <u>got its money from</u>, and what it has <u>done with it</u>. The two <u>balance out</u> exactly — hence the name. This page is about what the business <u>has done</u> with the money it's got.

It is calculated at a particular date — usually the <u>last day</u> of the <u>financial year</u>.

## Fixed Assets will Last for More Than One Year

1) The business has used some money to <u>buy fixed assets</u> — premises, machinery, vehicles.

2) This figure is what they're worth <u>on the date of the balance sheet</u> — they'll have <u>depreciated</u> since they were bought, but that's all taken care of in the <u>profit and loss account</u>.

## Current Assets Last a Few Months

These are listed in increasing <u>order of liquidity</u>:

1) <u>Stock</u> is the <u>least liquid</u>. It includes raw materials and finished products that the firm has <u>spent its money on</u> but which have <u>not yet been sold</u>.

2) <u>Debtors</u> refers to the value of <u>products sold</u> — usually on credit — that have <u>not yet been paid for</u> by the customers. What's happening here is that the firm is <u>lending its money</u> to customers so they can buy its products.

3) <u>Cash</u> is the most liquid. This is money the firm <u>hasn't spent</u> on anything yet — it's just <u>sitting in the bank</u>.

**BALANCE SHEET**
Yummo Chocolates Ltd., 31st March 2009

|  | £000 | £000 |
|---|---|---|
| **Fixed Assets** | | |
| Premises | | 80 |
| Machinery | | 40 |
| Vehicles | | 30 |
| | | 150 |
| **Current Assets** | | |
| Stock | 5 | |
| Debtors | 12 | |
| Cash | 3 | |
| | 20 | |
| **Current Liabilities** | | |
| Creditors | (14) | |
| Unpaid Corporation Tax | (1) | |
| | (15) | |
| Net Current Assets (Working Capital) | | 5 |
| Net Assets | | 155 |
| **Financed by** | | |
| **Shareholders' Funds** | | |
| Share Capital | | 80 |
| Retained Profit and Reserves | | 50 |
| **Long-term Liabilities** | | |
| Bank Loan | | 20 |
| Debentures | | 5 |
| Capital Employed | | 155 |

*Brackets around a number means it's <u>negative</u>.*

*Current Assets – Current Liabilities*

*Fixed Assets + Net Current Assets*

*The <u>liquidity</u> of an asset tells you how easy it is to convert into <u>money</u>.*

*This purple bit is the <u>Capital Employed</u> section — see the next page.*

## Current Liabilities are Bills the Firm Has to Pay Soon

1) These are any payments the firm will have to make <u>within one year</u> of the date on the balance sheet. <u>Creditors</u> is the opposite of debtors — it is money the <u>firm owes</u> to its <u>suppliers</u>. Also included is any <u>unpaid corporation tax</u> — payable to the government out of the previous year's profits — as well as any <u>unpaid dividends</u> to shareholders (there aren't any for Yummo this year, so this figure's not shown).

2) This is money which <u>doesn't really</u> belong to the firm, since it's going to have to pay it to <u>someone else</u> pretty soon. So you <u>take this away</u> from the current assets figure...

## Current Assets – Current Liabilities = Net Current Assets

1) The <u>net current assets</u> figure is what you get when you <u>subtract</u> those <u>current liabilities</u> from the <u>current assets</u>. It's also called <u>working capital</u>.

2) Add the <u>net current assets</u> to the <u>fixed assets</u> and you get the <u>net assets</u>, or net worth, of the business. This is the amount the firm would make if it <u>sold</u> all its assets (in theory) — it's what the firm is <u>worth</u>.

*Both these calculations are labelled on the balance sheet above.*

## Current assets — I'm more of a sultana guy myself...

I told you this was tricky. You're gonna finish this off on the <u>next page</u> — but it's definitely worth trying to make sure you've <u>understood everything</u> so far. Make sure you know the names of all the <u>headings</u> and their meanings, and that you understand why current liabilities are <u>taken away</u>.

# The Balance Sheet — Capital Employed

Now for the second part of the balance sheet — where did all the <u>money come from</u> to <u>create</u> the net worth of the business. Originally it came from <u>shareholders</u> buying the shares, and money <u>loaned to it</u> by other people — over the years this will be added to with <u>profit</u> that the firm has <u>retained</u>, and possibly <u>more loans</u>.

## Shareholders' Funds Came from the Firm's Owners

1) SHARE CAPITAL is the money put into the business when shares were <u>originally issued</u>. This might have been years and years ago for long-established companies.

   This is <u>not the same</u> as what the shares are <u>currently worth</u>. Most shares traded on the <u>stock exchange</u> are <u>second-hand</u> — the person selling them gets the cash, not the firm.

   Firms can raise <u>new capital</u> by issuing <u>new shares</u>. The usual way is to have a <u>rights issue</u>. This is where existing shareholders are offered new shares at a reduced price.

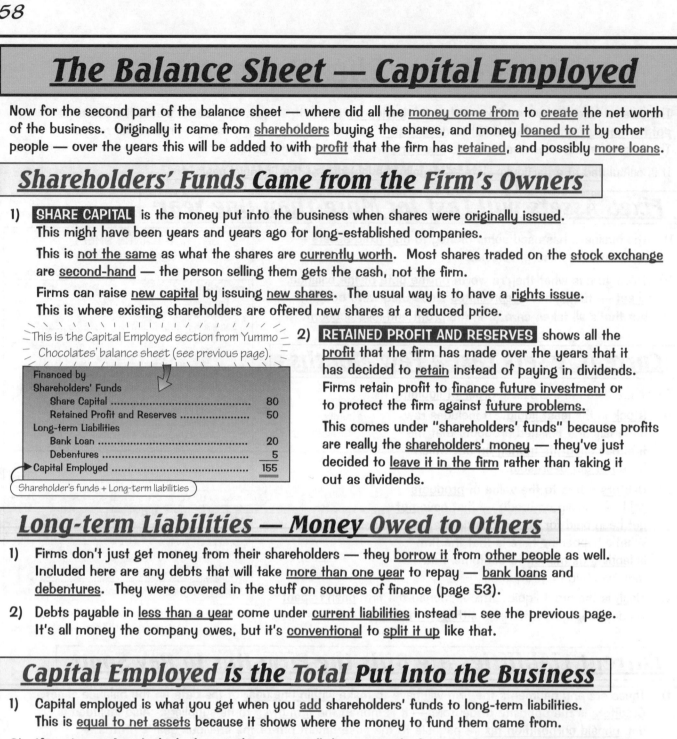

This is the Capital Employed section from Yummo Chocolates' balance sheet (see previous page).

```
Financed by
Shareholders' Funds
   Share Capital ........................    80
   Retained Profit and Reserves ......    50
Long-term Liabilities
   Bank Loan ...........................    20
   Debentures ..........................     5
Capital Employed .......................   155
```

Shareholder's funds + Long-term liabilities

2) RETAINED PROFIT AND RESERVES shows all the <u>profit</u> that the firm has made over the years that it has decided to <u>retain</u> instead of paying in dividends. Firms retain profit to <u>finance future investment</u> or to protect the firm against <u>future problems</u>.

   This comes under "shareholders' funds" because profits are really the <u>shareholders' money</u> — they've just decided to <u>leave it in the firm</u> rather than taking it out as dividends.

## Long-term Liabilities — Money Owed to Others

1) Firms don't just get money from their shareholders — they <u>borrow it</u> from <u>other people</u> as well. Included here are any debts that will take <u>more than one year</u> to repay — <u>bank loans</u> and <u>debentures</u>. They were covered in the stuff on sources of finance (page 53).

2) Debts payable in <u>less than a year</u> come under <u>current liabilities</u> instead — see the previous page. It's all money the company owes, but it's <u>conventional</u> to <u>split it up</u> like that.

## Capital Employed is the Total Put Into the Business

1) Capital employed is what you get when you <u>add</u> shareholders' funds to long-term liabilities. This is <u>equal to net assets</u> because it shows where the money to fund them came from.

2) If you're <u>confused</u>, think about it this way — all the money the business <u>has got</u> (from shareholders and borrowing from other people) is accounted for by <u>capital employed</u>. And everything it's <u>done with the money</u> it got (bought premises, kept it as cash, etc.) is listed under <u>net assets</u>. They have to be the <u>same</u> — because money <u>doesn't just vanish</u>.

## The Balance Sheet is Useful to Stakeholders

1) <u>Stakeholders</u> use the balance sheet to <u>assess</u> the financial health of a business.

2) The <u>net assets</u> figure from the balance sheet can show this. A business whose net assets are <u>growing</u> each year is probably <u>healthy</u>, because it's <u>increasing</u> the value of its fixed assets and its cash reserves.

3) On the other hand, a business with <u>low</u> or <u>negative</u> net assets may be <u>unhealthy</u>. It might be <u>borrowing</u> money to finance short-term assets — such as <u>unsold stock</u>, or debtors who may not pay their bills.

## Share capital — but I want to keep it all for myself...

These two pages are <u>worth struggling with</u> until you've understood all of it. Explain what all the <u>headings</u> mean — then make sure you can explain why the whole thing is called a <u>balance</u> sheet.

# Liquidity Ratios

Liquidity ratios tell you how <u>easy</u> it is for a business to pay off this year's <u>current liabilities</u> (i.e. this year's bills) using their <u>current assets</u> (money and existing stock).

## Current Ratio — also called the Working Capital Ratio

The middle part of a balance sheet shows a firm's <u>current assets</u> and <u>current liabilities</u>. ('Current' means 'this year', basically.)

> This is part of Yummo Chocolates' balance sheet from page 57.

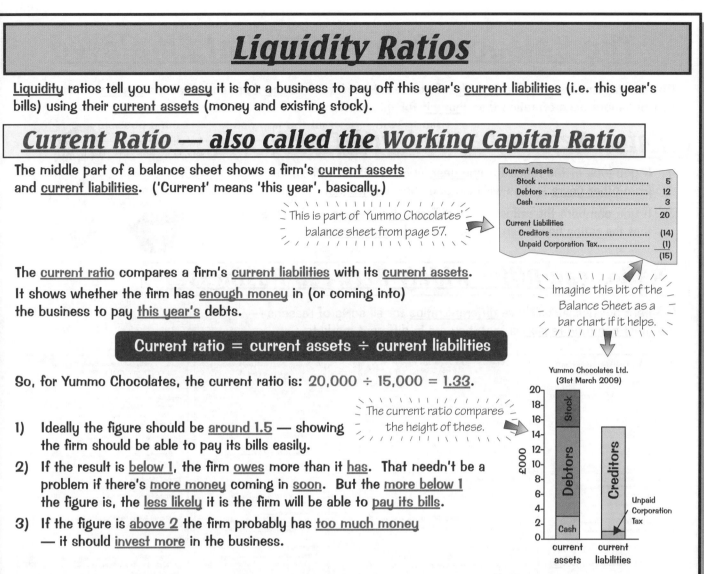

| Current Assets | |
| --- | --- |
| Stock ............................... | 5 |
| Debtors ............................ | 12 |
| Cash ................................ | 3 |
| | 20 |
| Current Liabilities | |
| Creditors .......................... | (14) |
| Unpaid Corporation Tax.......... | (1) |
| | (15) |

The <u>current ratio</u> compares a firm's <u>current liabilities</u> with its <u>current assets</u>. It shows whether the firm has <u>enough money</u> in (or coming into) the business to pay <u>this year's</u> debts.

> Imagine this bit of the Balance Sheet as a bar chart if it helps.

> **Current ratio = current assets ÷ current liabilities**

So, for Yummo Chocolates, the current ratio is: 20,000 ÷ 15,000 = <u>1.33</u>.

> The current ratio compares the height of these.

1) Ideally the figure should be <u>around 1.5</u> — showing the firm should be able to pay its bills easily.

2) If the result is <u>below 1</u>, the firm <u>owes</u> more than it <u>has</u>. That needn't be a problem if there's <u>more money</u> coming in <u>soon</u>. But the <u>more below 1</u> the figure is, the <u>less likely</u> it is the firm will be able to <u>pay its bills</u>.

3) If the figure is <u>above 2</u> the firm probably has <u>too much money</u> — it should <u>invest more</u> in the business.

The current ratio assumes that the company will be able to turn <u>stock</u> into <u>cash</u> during the year. Unfortunately, there are <u>no guarantees</u> it'll be able to do this. Which is why there's <u>another</u> ratio...

## Acid Test Ratio — also called the Liquid Capital Ratio

This is <u>similar</u> to the current ratio, but takes a slightly more pessimistic view of things. It assumes that the company <u>won't</u> be able to turn stock into cash (i.e. that it <u>won't</u> be able to sell its stock during the year).

> **Acid test ratio = (current assets − stock) ÷ current liabilities.**

So, for Yummo Chocolates, the current ratio is: (20,000 − 5,000) ÷ 15,000 = <u>1</u>.

The result will be <u>lower</u> than the <u>current ratio</u>, so the rules are different...

1) If the acid test ratio is <u>much above 1</u>, you've got too much <u>cash</u> lying about — it would be <u>more profitable</u> to <u>invest</u> this money.

2) If it's <u>much below 1</u>, you might be in schtuck.

LIVE TONIGHT...
The Assets

> The acid test ratio compares the height of these bars.

---

## If Venice was a capital city, I'd have a dead funny joke here...

Well, there you go — <u>liquidity ratios</u> done. Hurray hurrah. Make sure you know what are <u>good values</u> for the current ratio and the acid test ratio. Oh, and remember it's the acid test that <u>ignores</u> stock. Easy peasy.

# Analysis of Accounts

There's no point knowing the <u>formulas</u> if you don't know how to <u>use</u> them and what the <u>answers</u> mean. Just one more page on ratios then <u>that's it</u> for this section.

## Ratios Need to be Used With Care

1) If you look at the ratios for <u>one year</u>, compare them with ratios from <u>other years</u> — this will help you spot any <u>trends</u>.

2) If you compare the ratios of two <u>different businesses</u>, make sure that the ratios have been worked out in the <u>same way</u>.

> And our acid test ratio is... **1.54**

## Ratios can Differ Widely Between Businesses

Different businesses will have <u>different ratios</u> for all sorts of reasons — the <u>most common reason</u> is that they are in <u>different markets</u>.

### Trading, Profit and Loss Account for Clevercloggs Websites Plc — Year ending 31 March 2009

| | £000 | £000 |
|---|---|---|
| Turnover | | 120 |
| Minus cost of sales | | |
| Opening stock | 1 | |
| Purchases | 8 | |
| | 9 | |
| Minus closing stock | (2) | |
| | | (7) |
| Gross profit | | 113 |
| Minus expenses | | |
| Wages and salaries | 32 | |
| Rent and rates | 8 | |
| Office expenses | 8 | |
| Advertising | 30 | |
| Depreciation | 2 | |
| Other expenses | 5 | |
| | | (85) |
| Operating profit | | 28 |
| Interest payable | | (1) |
| Profit before taxation (net profit) | | 27 |
| Taxation | | (4) |
| Dividends | | (14) |
| Retained profit | | 9 |

### Balance Sheet for Clevercloggs Websites Plc — 31 March 2009

| | £000 | £000 |
|---|---|---|
| Fixed Assets | | |
| Premises | | 30 |
| Machinery | | 40 |
| Vehicles | | 18 |
| | | 88 |
| Current Assets | | |
| Stock | 2 | |
| Debtors | 6 | |
| Cash | 12 | |
| | 20 | |
| Current Liabilities | | |
| Creditors | (8) | |
| Unpaid Corporation Tax | (2) | |
| | (10) | |
| Net Current Assets (Working Capital) | | 10 |
| Net Assets | | 98 |
| Financed by | | |
| Shareholders Funds | | |
| Share Capital | | 16 |
| Retained Profit and Reserves | | 73 |
| Long-term Liabilities | | |
| Bank Loan | | 9 |
| Debentures | | 0 |
| Capital Employed | | 98 |

### Trading, Profit and Loss Account for Naturo Pong Plc — Year ending 31 March 2009

| | £m | £m |
|---|---|---|
| Turnover | | 780 |
| Minus cost of sales | | |
| Opening stock | 89 | |
| Purchases | 420 | |
| | 509 | |
| Minus closing stock | (75) | |
| | | (434) |
| Gross profit | | 346 |
| Minus expenses | | |
| Wages and salaries | 93 | |
| Rent and rates | 75 | |
| Office expenses | 35 | |
| Advertising | 5 | |
| Depreciation | 35 | |
| Other expenses | 68 | |
| | | (311) |
| Operating profit | | 35 |
| Interest payable | | (20) |
| Profit before taxation (net profit) | | 15 |
| Taxation | | (2) |
| Dividends | | (9) |
| Retained profit | | 4 |

### Balance Sheet for Naturo Pong Plc — 31 March 2009

| | £m | £m |
|---|---|---|
| Fixed Assets | | |
| Premises | | 550 |
| Machinery | | 250 |
| Vehicles | | 6 |
| | | 806 |
| Current Assets | | |
| Stock | 75 | |
| Debtors | 45 | |
| Cash | 12 | |
| | 132 | |
| Current Liabilities | | |
| Creditors | (62) | |
| Unpaid Corporation Tax | (10) | |
| | (72) | |
| Net Current Assets (Working Capital) | | 60 |
| Net Assets | | 866 |
| Financed by | | |
| Shareholders Funds | | |
| Share Capital | | 560 |
| Retained Profit and Reserves | | 126 |
| Long-term Liabilities | | |
| Bank Loan | | 140 |
| Debentures | | 40 |
| Capital Employed | | 866 |

### Ratios for Clevercloggs Websites Plc.
Gross Profit Margin = 94.17%
Net Profit Margin = 22.5%
Acid Test = 1.8

### Ratios for Naturo Pong Plc.
Gross Profit Margin = 44.36%
Net Profit Margin = 1.92%
Acid Test = 0.79

● Clevercloggs is an <u>internet</u> firm so it <u>doesn't make anything</u>. Its main expenses are its computers and an office. As a result its <u>gross profit margin</u> is <u>very high</u>.

● Its <u>acid test</u> is <u>too high</u> — it should <u>invest</u> some of its <u>unused cash</u>.

It definitely looks like this business should invest some of its unused cash.

● Naturo Pong is a <u>capital-intensive</u> <u>manufacturer</u>. It sells into a <u>competitive</u> market where <u>low prices</u> help firms sell their product. Its <u>high gross profit margin</u> but <u>low net profit margin</u> reflect the <u>high fixed costs</u> of a chemicals manufacturer.

● Its <u>net profit margin</u> and <u>acid test</u> are very low — that should be <u>extremely worrying</u> for the company's managers.

## Acid test — dip your finger in some and see if it hurts...

Check that you can see where the <u>answers</u> for the ratios came from. Make sure you know <u>why</u> the two businesses have such <u>different ratios</u> — and why <u>last year's</u> figures would be interesting.

# Revision Summary for Section Eight

Hurrah — I bet it's a relief to get to the end of that Section. Loads of nasty calculations and whatnot. Although, as the saying almost never goes — with great joy comes great responsibility. It's time for you to make sure you know all the juicy details of this section, and you should know what that means by now — a lovely revision summary (with numerical answers at the bottom, for use only once you've tried the questions yourself)...

1) Name two sources of finance that are only available to limited firms.

2) For each of the sources in question 1), identify one drawback of using this source of finance.

3) Explain why the state of the economy may affect the type of finance a firm chooses to use.

4) In a trading, profit and loss account, how do you calculate the cost of sales figure?

5) How is gross profit calculated in a trading, profit and loss account?

6) A gym buys a new treadmill for £3000. It's owner decides to depreciate it using the straight-line method, and assumes it will last for six years before it needs replacing. What allowance for depreciation will be in the accounts each year?

7) Is net profit calculated before or after tax is paid?

8) What type of business needs to complete an appropriation account? What does this account show?

9) Name three groups of people who might look at a firm's profit and loss account.

10) In 2009, a tiling business made a gross profit of £6000 and had sales of £24,000. What was the firm's gross profit margin?

11) Explain what the net profit margin represents.

12) What does a firm's balance sheet show?

13) Decide if each of the following is a fixed asset or a current asset:
   a) business premises   b) unsold stock   c) a fleet of company vehicles

14) Put these in order, most liquid first: debtors, stock, cash, mango purée (only kidding about the purée).

15) What are current liabilities?

16) What do you get if you deduct current liabilities from current assets?

17) What are the two types of shareholder funds shown on the balance sheet?

18) What is included under the heading 'long-term liabilities' on a balance sheet?

19) What is the term for describing all the money that has been put into the business?

20) Explain why the balance sheet is useful to a firm's stakeholders.

21) What do you get if you take away stock from current assets, and divide by current liabilities?
   a) current ratio;  b) acid test ratio;  c) a migraine.

22) Explain how the current ratio and the acid test ratio are different.

23) What is the ideal figure for the acid test ratio? Why is this so?

24) Look at the information on the right, and work out these ratios:
   a) current ratio;  b) acid test ratio.

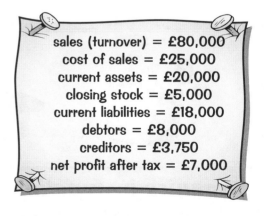

sales (turnover) = £80,000
cost of sales = £25,000
current assets = £20,000
closing stock = £5,000
current liabilities = £18,000
debtors = £8,000
creditors = £3,750
net profit after tax = £7,000

6) £500.
19) 0.25 or 25%.
25) a) 1.11;  b) 0.83.

# Organisational Structure

There are three main ways a business can structure its organisation. However you do it, you end up with a diagram that looks slightly like an upside-down tree. Hence the name "organisation tree".

## ① You Can Organise by Function...

1) You get this a lot in limited companies.

2) Each functional area does one part of the work of the business. Examples of functional areas are sales, marketing, customer service, operations, finance, human resources... and so on.

3) The main advantage is that specialists can concentrate on their particular job.

4) The main disadvantage is that the different departments may not work well together.

**Anyfirm Ltd.**

Neil Beforme — Managing Director

Ivor Nidea — Marketing Director | Justine Tyme — Production Director | Andy Wifiggis — Finance Director | Olive Sackenham — Personnel Director

Ewan Htwhen — Production Manager | Ian Eresumwear — Warehouse Manager | Mike Goodan-Mend — Repairs Manager

## ② ...You Can Organise by Product...

**Buy It All plc**

Buy It All plc

Home furnishings | Toys | Clothing

1) This is common with large manufacturers who make lots of different products.

2) A product-based structure splits the organisation into different sectors. For example, Buy-It-All PLC has three sectors — home furnishings, toys and clothing.

3) The main advantage is that managers can make decisions that are relevant to each product sector.

4) A disadvantage is that there can be a wasteful duplication of resources between sectors.

## ③ ...Or You Can Organise by Region

1) This is normal for a multinational business.

2) The divisions may be regional or national.

3) The main advantage is that spreading management between regions makes day-to-day control easier.

4) A disadvantage is that there can be a wasteful duplication of resources between regions.

**Megabucks (Global) plc**

Megabucks (Global) plc

Megabucks (North America) | Megabucks (Europe) | Megabucks (Asia)

Loadsamoney (UK) | Argent Grand (France) | Grosse Gelde (Deutschland)

Hmm... I'm sure that structure's wrong...

Workers → Bosses

No single structure is right for every business. Individual businesses need to decide what will suit them best.

## Organise by function — sort it out at a posh party...

Basically you've got three diagrams to learn. Make sure you can draw each one from memory. Remember that individual businesses have to find a structure that works for them — it could be any of these three.

# Organisational Structure

The amount of <u>authority</u> each person in an organisation has is determined by their place in the <u>hierarchy</u>...

## Businesses are Organised into Hierarchies

1) A <u>hierarchy</u> is a series of <u>levels</u> within the business, where each level has <u>responsibility</u> and <u>authority</u> over the levels <u>below</u>.

2) Generally, the number of people at each level <u>decreases</u> as you move <u>up</u> the hierarchy.

3) At each level, a certain amount of responsibility is <u>delegated</u> (passed on) to people in the level <u>below</u>.

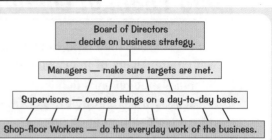

Board of Directors — decide on business strategy.
Managers — make sure targets are met.
Supervisors — oversee things on a day-to-day basis.
Shop-floor Workers — do the everyday work of the business.

## Organisations can be Centralised or Decentralised

<u>How much</u> power and authority is <u>delegated</u> at each level in the hierarchy will depend on whether the bosses want a <u>centralised</u> or <u>decentralised</u> structure.

### Centralised Organisations

1) <u>All major decisions</u> are made by one person or a few senior managers at the <u>top</u> of the hierarchy.

2) <u>Advantages</u> are that these senior managers tend to have plenty of <u>experience</u>, and can get an <u>overview</u> of the whole business. Policies will be <u>uniform</u> throughout the business.

3) On the <u>downside</u>, if all decisions need to be made by one or two people, it can <u>slow down</u> decision-making. Decisions can also take a <u>long time</u> to filter through to employees. This means that the organisation reacts <u>slowly</u> to change.

4) Senior managers at the top of a hierarchy can become <u>very powerful</u>. But depending too heavily on a few people at the top can cause problems if those people <u>lack specialist knowledge</u> or if they 'lose their touch' and start making poor decisions.

### Decentralised Organisations

1) The authority to make most decisions is <u>shared out</u> — for example, power might be delegated to <u>regional managers</u> or to more <u>junior employees</u>.

2) <u>Advantages</u> are that employees can use <u>expert knowledge</u> of their sector to make decisions, and these decisions can be made more <u>quickly</u>.

3) The <u>disadvantages</u> are that <u>inconsistencies</u> may develop between departments or regions. Also, the decision makers might not be able to see the <u>overall</u> needs of the business.

## The Structure of a Business Can Change Over Time

1) Businesses tend to become <u>more hierarchical</u> as they get larger (i.e. their hierarchy develops more <u>layers</u>).

2) A small business is often run by just the owner without any help. As the business grows and employs more staff, <u>managers</u> might be needed to help <u>organise</u> and <u>control</u> things.

3) The <u>bigger</u> the business, the greater the number of <u>managers</u> needed (and the greater the <u>costs</u>).

4) To overcome this, some businesses <u>delayer</u> their structure — layers of management are <u>removed</u> (usually from the <u>middle</u> of the hierarchy). They may also <u>decentralise</u> their organisation and encourage groups of workers to take <u>more responsibility</u> for their own self-management.

## Decentralisation — popular in the doughnut industry...

Make sure you understand the terms <u>hierarchy</u>, <u>centralised</u> and <u>decentralised</u>, and you know the <u>pros</u> and <u>cons</u> of being a centralised and decentralised organisation. Remember — firms often start out with a centralised structure, but are forced to decentralise as they get <u>too big</u> to make all the decisions at the top.

# Effects of Expansion — Communication

You've already seen a bit about <u>organisational structure</u> on pages 62-63. But now you need to know how a business's structure can cause <u>problems</u> for communication, especially as the business grows.

## A Long Chain of Communication is a Problem...

1) As firms grow, they tend to become more <u>hierarchical</u>, with many <u>layers of management</u>.

2) A <u>chain of communication</u> in a firm is the chain of people messages travel through to get from <u>one layer</u> of the firm's hierarchy to <u>another</u>.

3) Here, Dodgy Computers has six levels in its hierarchy, so its <u>longest</u> chain of communication (from the <u>top</u> of the hierarchy to the <u>bottom</u>) has six layers.

4) Long chains of communication mean messages can take a <u>long time</u> to travel up and down the hierarchy. This can leave people at the top and the bottom of the hierarchy feeling <u>isolated</u> and demoralised. There's also the danger that messages may not reach their intended destination — and even if they do, they might get <u>distorted</u> along the way (like in a game of Chinese whispers).

5) Some firms have tried to <u>solve the problem</u> of long chains of communication by <u>de-layering</u> — removing tiers of management, usually in the middle.

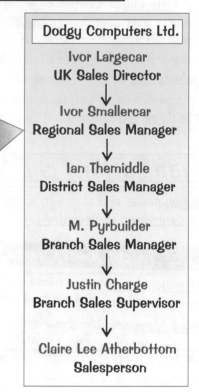

**Dodgy Computers Ltd.**

Ivor Largecar
**UK Sales Director**
↓
Ivor Smallercar
**Regional Sales Manager**
↓
Ian Themiddle
**District Sales Manager**
↓
M. Pyrbuilder
**Branch Sales Manager**
↓
Justin Charge
**Branch Sales Supervisor**
↓
Claire Lee Atherbottom
**Salesperson**

## ...and so is a Wide Span of Control

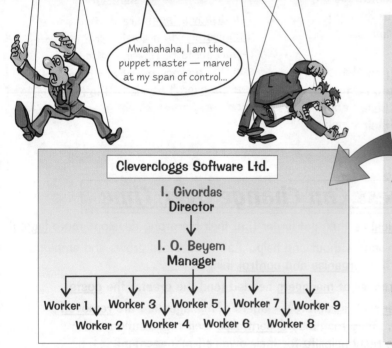

Mwahahaha, I am the puppet master — marvel at my span of control...

**Cleverclogs Software Ltd.**

I. Givordas
**Director**
↓
I. O. Beyem
**Manager**
↓
Worker 1  Worker 3  Worker 5  Worker 7  Worker 9
Worker 2  Worker 4  Worker 6  Worker 8

1) The <u>span of control</u> is the number of workers who report to <u>one</u> manager in a hierarchy.

2) The manager of Cleverclogs Software has a span of control of <u>nine</u> workers.

3) A <u>wide</u> span of control leads to a manager having to communicate with a <u>lot</u> of employees.

4) This means it can take a <u>long time</u> to pass messages to all the people under a manager's control (and for them all to pass messages back to the manager). It can also be <u>difficult</u> to manage a lot of employees <u>effectively</u>.

5) Firms must find <u>balance</u> between a <u>short</u> chain of communication and a <u>narrow</u> span of control.

## Spam of control — managers sending hundreds of emails...

A good page this, I reckon — not too much to learn and a couple of pretty diagrams to look at.
A firm needs to achieve a <u>balance</u> between its <u>span of control</u> and <u>chain of communication</u>.
If the span is too wide, or the chain is too long, <u>communication</u> within the business could start to <u>suffer</u>.

# Staff Training

Right, now listen up... you should already know about <u>recruitment</u> (see pages 26–27 if you've forgotten). But once staff have been recruited, they need to learn <u>how to do their jobs</u> — that's where <u>training</u> comes in.

## Induction Training is for New Staff

1) Induction training <u>introduces</u> the new employee to their workplace. It usually starts on the <u>first day</u> of the new job.

2) It includes introducing them to their <u>fellow workers</u> and telling them about <u>company rules</u> — including <u>health and safety</u> rules. They should be given a <u>tour</u> of the site so they don't get lost. It may also include some initial training on <u>how to do</u> their new job.

3) It should help to make the new employee feel <u>welcome</u> and <u>comfortable</u> in their new place of work.

## On-the-Job Training is Learning by Doing

1) This is the <u>most common</u> form of training. The person learns to do their job better by being <u>shown how to do it</u> — and then <u>practising</u>. It is also sometimes called <u>internal training</u>.

2) It is <u>cost-effective</u> for the employer because the person <u>continues to work</u> while learning.

3) A problem is that it is often <u>taught by a colleague</u> — so <u>bad working practices</u> can be passed on.

Yeah, we're supposed to lock the safe every night, but we never actually bother.

## Off-the-Job Training can be Internal or External

1) This happens when the person learns <u>away</u> from their <u>workplace</u>. If the firm has its own training department, off-the-job training can be done <u>internally</u> (or <u>in-house</u>). Training that happens <u>outside</u> the business is called <u>external training</u> — for example, a course at a college.

2) It's more <u>expensive</u> than on-the-job training, and sometimes not as <u>directly related</u> to the actual job. But it's often <u>higher quality</u> because it's taught by people who are better qualified to train others.

## Appraisal Helps to Identify Training Needs

The <u>appraisal</u> process helps managers to keep track of employees' progress and needs. There are <u>three stages</u>:

**1** The worker and their manager agree the worker's <u>performance targets</u> for the year. → **2** During the year, training and other resources are provided to help the worker <u>meet the targets</u>. → **3** At the end of the year they meet again to discuss <u>how well</u> the targets were <u>met</u>.

Then the process starts all over again...

1) People who <u>meet or beat</u> their targets could be <u>rewarded</u> with higher pay or a promotion. If a worker <u>does not meet</u> their targets, the manager can decide what action to take to help them <u>improve</u>.

2) Appraisal meetings can cause <u>problems</u> if they're <u>badly managed</u>. If a worker's targets <u>aren't realistic</u> they probably won't meet them — this can <u>demotivate</u> staff. And lack of <u>honesty</u> can be a problem — employees sometimes just say what they think managers want to hear, while some managers just try to avoid upsetting people.

## It's training, men — hallelujah...

Your teachers can't really expect you to get your GCSEs without teaching you something first. It's the same in business — a company can't expect staff to do their jobs <u>properly</u> without training. Easy.

# Staff Motivation and Retention

Keeping staff <u>motivated</u> is important for any business. Workers want to feel <u>valued</u> and that they're doing their jobs well. This page covers some of the ways that businesses fill their staff with <u>happiness and joy</u>.

## Staff Can be Motivated with Remuneration

Only 15 days, 5 hours and 13 minutes till pay-day...

Paying staff <u>money</u> for the work they do is called <u>remuneration</u> — or <u>financial reward</u>.

1) Unless they're volunteers, most workers earn a basic <u>wage</u> or <u>salary</u> for doing their job. <u>Increasing</u> this wage or salary can help to motivate staff — it means they have <u>more money</u> to spend on the things they enjoy.

2) Other types of remuneration include <u>bonuses</u> and <u>pension payments</u> (see page 28).

3) Larger businesses usually have more money to spend on remuneration for staff. For example, a <u>growing</u> business is <u>more likely</u> to offer a yearly bonus than a <u>small</u> business.

4) As it <u>grows</u>, a firm will often offer its staff <u>more</u> financial rewards on top of their basic pay.

## Training Can Also Boost Motivation

1) The main point of training is to make staff <u>better at their jobs</u>. Staff who are good at their jobs are generally <u>better motivated</u> (see page 29).

2) As staff learn new skills through training, they may be <u>promoted</u> to jobs higher up in the business. The <u>extra pay</u> and <u>responsibility</u> that come with a promotion are often good for staff motivation.

3) Training can also help staff meet their <u>personal targets</u> as part of the appraisal process.

## Motivation Can be Affected by Styles of Management

1) <u>Authoritarian</u> (or <u>autocratic</u>) managers make decisions <u>alone</u>, without consulting staff.

2) <u>Paternalistic</u> managers make decisions <u>themselves</u>, but only after <u>consultation</u> with workers.

3) <u>Democratic</u> managers allow the workforce some <u>influence</u> over decisions.

4) <u>Laissez-faire</u> managers allow workers to perform tasks as they see fit, offering help if needed.

<u>No single</u> approach is perfect for <u>all</u> employees and <u>all</u> situations. For example...

• The authoritarian style can make workers feel their views <u>aren't valued</u> — which can demotivate able staff.

• At the other end of the scale, laissez-faire management leaves workers to work things out for themselves — great for independent, motivated workers, but it could be a <u>problem</u> for staff who need support.

• In larger businesses with lots of managers, staff may have to <u>adapt</u> to a different style on a regular basis.

## Staff Retention is About Keeping Hold of Good Workers

1) All businesses invest <u>time</u> and <u>money</u> in recruiting and training their staff.

2) For <u>large businesses</u>, recruitment (see pages 26-27) can be a major task — there may be <u>hundreds</u> of application forms to process. And interviewing and testing the shortlisted candidates could take <u>days</u>.

3) If employees are <u>good</u> at their jobs, businesses will want to <u>retain</u> them for <u>as long as possible</u> — otherwise they'll have to find <u>replacements</u>. This means more recruitment and training.

4) <u>Motivation</u> can help with staff retention — well-motivated staff are less likely to want to leave their jobs.

5) Many large businesses aim to retain staff by offering a <u>career path</u>. In a large firm, there are plenty of opportunities for <u>promotion</u> — employees have an incentive to stay and work their way up the <u>hierarchy</u>.

## That paternalistic manager is the daddy around here...

There's nothing surprising about this — happy staff are <u>more productive</u> than miserable staff, and they're likely to <u>stay in their jobs</u> for longer. <u>Managers</u> play an important role in keeping staff motivated.

# Revision Summary for Section Nine

This section is all about people — how to organise them, how to train them, and how to keep them happy and motivated so that they won't want to find a job somewhere else.

If you're reading this, chances are that you're a person — so answering all these questions about people should be a piece of cake, right? If it's not, you probably need to do some more revision on this section.

1) What are the three main ways that businesses can be structured?

2) Give one advantage and one disadvantage of each type of structure you listed in question 1.

3) Say which type of structure would be most suitable for these companies:
   a) a transnational oil company with offices all over the world;
   b) a limited company that manufactures washing machine parts.

4) Explain what is meant by a business hierarchy.

5) Describe the differences between a centralised and a decentralised organisation.

6) Give one advantage and one disadvantage that a centralised structure has for a business.
   Then do the same for a decentralised structure.

7) Describe how the structure of a business typically changes as the business grows.

8) Explain what is meant by delayering.

9) What does 'span of control' mean? And why might a wide span of control be a problem in a business?

10) Explain how a firm's chain of communication is related to its hierarchy.

11) How can a long chain of communication cause problems for a business?

12) What should happen during induction training? And when does it usually start?

13) Explain the difference between on-the-job and off-the-job training.

14) Give one advantage and one disadvantage of on-the-job training.

15) Describe the three stages of the appraisal process.

16) Explain two potential problems with the appraisal process.

17) What is remuneration, and how can it help to motivate staff?

18) Explain two ways that training may help to motivate staff.

19) If you make decisions alone, but only after consulting your staff, what type of manager are you?
    a) Authoritarian;  b) Paternalistic;  c) Democratic;  d) Quite nice.

20) What's the main potential problem with the laissez-faire management style?

21) Explain what 'staff retention' means.

22) Explain one method a large business might use to maximise staff retention.

# Specialisation and Interdependence

Specialisation is a <u>simple idea</u> — if I'm good at cooking but can't count, and you're good at accounting but your cooking stinks, then our catering business will do <u>much better</u> if I do all the cooking and you do all the accounting. It's a lot <u>more sensible</u> than us both spending half our time on each.

## Specialisation Leads to Division of Labour

Firms use <u>specialisation</u> to make their production more efficient. It's called <u>division of labour</u> — that means they divide up their workers and get each one of them to do a <u>specific job</u>.

1) Workers can <u>play to their strengths</u> — you might be a naturally gifted brain surgeon, say, or a drummer.

2) Skills are <u>improved</u>. If you spend all your time doing brain surgery or drumming, you get better.

3) Firms always try to <u>break up</u> complex production techniques into a series of <u>simple tasks</u>, and get workers to <u>specialise</u> in those tasks.

4) Workers may do the same task hundreds of times a day — so they get very <u>efficient</u> at it. And this improves the firm's <u>productivity</u>.

## Division of Labour has its Problems

It's not all good news, though. Often you have to specialise in something more <u>boring</u> than brain surgery, like screwing the <u>same little bolt</u> onto an <u>endless</u> production line of mopeds.

1) Workers may get <u>bored</u> doing the same thing every day — resulting in <u>low job satisfaction</u>.

2) This can lead to <u>poor quality</u> products, more <u>absenteeism</u> and frequent <u>industrial action</u>.

3) A problem with <u>one group</u> of workers may halt production in the <u>whole business</u>.

4) Workers can become <u>over-specialised</u> — they might have difficulty finding another job if their skills are no longer in demand. Unemployment due to <u>occupational immobility</u> may result.

## Specialisation Makes Firms Interdependent

It's not just <u>workers in firms</u> who specialise. <u>Firms themselves</u> specialise too. One firm will grow cocoa, another will process it, another will ship it. One firm will make chocolate bars, another will sell them. You generally <u>don't</u> get <u>one</u> firm trying to do <u>all</u> these things — firms specialise in what they're <u>best</u> at. This makes the whole process more <u>efficient</u>.

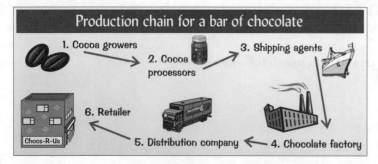

Production chain for a bar of chocolate

1. Cocoa growers
2. Cocoa processors
3. Shipping agents
4. Chocolate factory
5. Distribution company
6. Retailer
Chocs-R-Us

Firms are <u>interdependent</u> with businesses in the same <u>production chain</u>. If there's a crisis in the cocoa-growing industry, Chocs-R-Us are in trouble too.

Some production stages make the product <u>more valuable</u> than before — this is called <u>adding value</u>. Other stages of production provide vital <u>services</u> (for example, transporting the product).

## Division of labour — but the Tories aren't united either...

This is a <u>seriously important</u> page. Without division of labour we'd <u>all</u> be a lot poorer. It was ideas about <u>efficiency</u> like these that spawned the age of <u>mass manufacturing</u>, and led to huge <u>economic growth</u>. Just think... if it wasn't for mass manufacturing, things like PCs would still be made in small mountain workshops by the local clockmaker — like they must have been in the old days. Aye, it was all different then.

# Methods of Production

Growing businesses may need to <u>increase</u> their production to meet demand from their customers. But they also need to stay <u>efficient</u> so that they can keep their prices low. Here's how it's done...

## Flow Production is <u>Making Lots of Things Continuously</u>

<u>Flow production</u> enables businesses to make products <u>non-stop</u>. <u>Assembly lines</u> are the classic way to organise flow production. The whole factory is built around a <u>conveyor belt</u> which carries the product along — workers perform <u>set tasks</u> as the product travels past.

1) The aim of <u>flow production</u> is to make as many <u>identical</u> products as possible. To be <u>efficient</u>, production has to be <u>continuous</u> with no stoppages — many flow production factories operate 24 hours a day with workers rotating in <u>shifts</u>.

2) The aim is to gain from <u>economies of scale</u> (see p71) and so produce at <u>minimum unit cost</u> to allow <u>competitive</u> prices. Modern flow production techniques use <u>robots</u>, not people, to do most of the work. Flow production is highly <u>capital intensive</u> (it needs a lot of <u>money</u> up front — e.g. to buy machinery).

3) It's often used for <u>mass-market</u> products. Most modern consumer goods are produced this way — examples include <u>chocolate bars</u>, <u>mobile phones</u> and <u>televisions</u>.

4) Flow production is also sometimes called <u>mass</u> production.

## Businesses Can Produce <u>More Efficiently as They Grow</u>

1) Businesses aim to use the most <u>efficient</u> production methods possible.

2) Using job production and batch production (see p32) can make good sense for certain firms making particular products. But for <u>mass-market</u> products, <u>flow production</u> is usually the way to go.

3) Flow production takes the ideas of <u>specialisation</u> and <u>division of labour</u> (p68) to their extreme. Nowadays, vast robot-operated <u>production lines</u> can work around the clock. And because fewer workers are needed, <u>wage costs</u> can be lower.

4) As long as you can <u>sell</u> all these identical products (and can afford the potentially huge <u>initial investment</u>), flow production will be <u>more efficient</u> than job or batch production in the long run.

5) But this specialisation can easily lead to a lack of <u>flexibility</u>. <u>Switching production</u> from one product to another could mean stopping the production line and <u>retooling</u> it — resulting in very inefficient <u>downtime</u>.

6) However, as a business grows, it may be able to afford <u>larger premises</u>, and <u>more</u> production lines to manufacture different goods <u>simultaneously</u>. Or it may be able to invest in better, more adaptable <u>machinery</u> that can more easily <u>switch</u> from making one product to another.

## The secret of efficient production? Just go with the flow...

Flow production is great for churning out <u>huge numbers</u> of identical products. It means that large firms can keep up with demand for their products and keep their prices <u>low</u>. Bow down to your new robot masters.

# Productivity

Lean production is another strategy businesses can use to make themselves more efficient.
But first you need to know about production methods that aren't as lean as they could be...

## Two "Non-Lean" Stock Control Methods...

1) A traditional method is to use stock control graphs.
   - Here the firm has set the re-order level at 1000 widgets.
   - When stocks fall to 1000 widgets they will re-order 500 more.
   - The hope is that by the time the new stock arrives the firm's stock level won't have fallen below the minimum level.

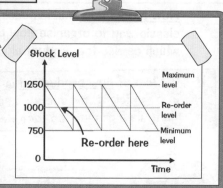

*A computerised stock control system can calculate stock levels and place orders automatically.*

2) Just-in-case (JIC) is a method of operating a production and distribution system with buffer stocks of items at every stage of the process — from raw materials to finished products — just in case there is a supply shortage or customer demand increases unexpectedly.
   - The idea is that even if there's a problem with deliveries of any raw materials, the buffer stocks will mean there can still be continuous production.
   - The main problem is that firms can be left with big stockpiles of items.

*JIC has tended to be replaced by JIT (see below) and other stock control methods.*

## Lean Production Uses as Few Resources as Possible

Lean production is a Japanese approach to making products that aims to use as few resources as possible. Waste and stocks of raw materials are kept to a minimum and workers are encouraged to think about ways to improve their productivity. The "Just-in-Time" method of stock control is a form of lean production.

Just-in-time (JIT) is a method that aims to keep stock levels to the bare minimum — ideally zero.
- The aim is that stock arrives in the factory immediately before it is used.
- The main benefit is that it reduces the cost of having to keep stocks (you need less warehouse space, fewer warehouse workers, and so on).
- The main problem is that it requires a lot of coordination between the firm and its suppliers — otherwise the firm could run out of stock.
- Extra training might be needed if JIT is to be successful.
- Another problem with JIT is some workers find it stressful if they are always on the verge of running out of stock. Some workers have called the system "Just too late".

## Rationalisation — Reorganising to Increase Efficiency

1) This is another method that firms can use to increase efficiency. Firms use rationalisation when they need to reduce overhead costs in order to reduce their break-even point.
2) Methods include
   - closing an administrative department and delegating their work elsewhere
   - closing a factory and moving the production to another site
   - reducing the number of managers
3) Rationalisation can be bad news for some workers as it often results in redundancies.

## Revise Just-in-time — not two weeks after the exam...

Don't be put off by all the text above — there's nothing that's totally impossible to learn about this page.
The main thing is to know how all the various methods work to improve the efficiency of a business.

# Effects of Expansion — Economies of Scale

One of the main <u>advantages</u> of expansion is the reductions in <u>average cost</u> that come from producing on a <u>large scale</u>. These are called <u>economies of scale</u> — and examiners are always <u>banging on</u> about how kids know nothing about this stuff, so give it a <u>good read</u> and show them that <u>you do</u>. Yeah, that'll teach 'em.

## There are Six Main Internal Economies of Scale

1) <u>PURCHASING ECONOMIES</u> happen when a <u>large firm</u> buys its supplies <u>in bulk</u> and so gets them at a cheaper unit price than a small firm.

But it's much cheaper to buy them in bulk...

2) <u>MARKETING ECONOMIES</u> arise because the cost of an <u>advertising campaign</u> is pretty much a <u>fixed cost</u>. A larger firm will need to spend <u>less per unit</u> advertising its products than a smaller firm.

3) <u>MANAGERIAL ECONOMIES</u> occur when a large firm can afford to employ <u>specialist managers</u> who have expert knowledge, such as <u>accountants</u> and <u>lawyers</u>.

4) <u>FINANCIAL ECONOMIES</u> result from <u>banks</u> being prepared to <u>lend more money</u> to larger firms at <u>lower interest rates</u>. This is because the banks know that larger firms are more likely to <u>pay them back</u> than smaller firms (see page 20).

5) <u>TECHNICAL ECONOMIES</u> occur because a large firm can afford to operate <u>more advanced machinery</u> than smaller firms. Also, the <u>law of increased dimensions</u> means that, for example, a factory that's ten times as <u>big</u> will be <u>less than</u> ten times as <u>expensive</u>.

6) <u>RISK-BEARING ECONOMIES</u> are where the firm can afford to sell a <u>range of products</u> into many <u>different markets</u>. A decline in sales of one product will not significantly harm the firm's cash flow (see p48).

## There are Four Main External Economies of Scale

These happen when a number of <u>large firms</u> locate <u>near to each other</u>.

1) When this happens <u>suppliers</u> will choose to locate <u>near their customers</u>. This reduces delivery times, transport costs and the need for the producers to hold large stocks of raw materials.

2) There will be a <u>local workforce</u> who already have the <u>skills needed</u> — they learned them working for other firms in the area. This reduces <u>training costs</u> for the firms.

3) The area will build up a <u>good reputation</u> for particular products. This will <u>benefit</u> firms in the area and <u>encourage</u> other firms to locate there.

4) <u>Local councils</u> and <u>national government</u> may also encourage large businesses to move to or stay in a particular area — e.g. grants may be made available.

## But There are also Diseconomies of Scale

It's not all good news for large firms though — growth brings with it some <u>diseconomies of scale</u>:

1) The <u>bigger</u> the firm the <u>harder</u> it is to <u>manage</u> it properly.

2) Decisions <u>take time</u> to reach the whole workforce, and workers at the bottom of the hierarchy feel <u>insignificant</u>. Workers can get <u>demotivated</u>, which may cause <u>productivity</u> to go down.

3) The <u>production process</u> may become <u>more complex</u> and more difficult to <u>coordinate</u>. This means <u>different departments</u> may end up working on very <u>similar</u> projects without knowing.

## Economy of scale — buying fish by the truckload...

This might seem a bit tricky at first, but it's not too bad. Basically, <u>bigger firms</u> can <u>produce goods</u> at a <u>lower cost per item</u>. And it's that <u>per item</u> bit that's important. Make sure you go over this page until it's all clear — examiners love asking you about this stuff and you don't need me to tell you it's a <u>good idea</u> to know it.

# Quality Management

Customers expect businesses to provide a <u>decent level</u> of quality, so businesses need to have some way of ensuring that the goods or services they're providing are <u>up to scratch</u>. But as a firm gets more and more successful and needs to produce more and more, it can get harder and harder to maintain <u>high standards</u>.

## Quality Control — Spotting Problems Before it's Too Late

1) Quality control involves <u>checking products</u> to make sure quality standards are being met. This used to be done by quality inspectors, but some firms now encourage workers to <u>check their own quality</u>.

2) Products are checked for things like <u>design</u>, <u>appearance</u>, <u>defects</u> and <u>safety</u>, usually at <u>three different stages</u> of the production process. The <u>aim</u> is to stop faulty goods from reaching the customer.

| STAGE 1 | STAGE 2 | STAGE 3 |
|---|---|---|
| Check <u>raw materials</u> from suppliers. | Random samples taken to check quality of <u>work in progress</u>. | Random samples taken of <u>finished products</u> — items removed if they don't meet required quality. |

3) Defects are spotted <u>as they happen</u> rather than waiting until products are finished — this reduces waste.

4) Quality control can be <u>expensive</u> (sometimes whole <u>batches</u> of goods might need to be scrapped). But the cost to the business would be <u>greater</u> if dissatisfied customers stopped buying their products.

## Total Quality Management — a Culture of Quality

1) The <u>Total Quality Management</u> (TQM) strategy aims to make quality the responsibility of <u>every</u> employee in an organisation. Employees are encouraged to think about the needs of the customer. The emphasis is on <u>getting things right first time</u> — this <u>reduces</u> costs by cutting down on waste.

2) <u>Quality circles</u> are an important TQM feature. <u>Groups of workers</u> from various departments meet regularly to identify quality problems and offer solutions — this can lead to <u>increased motivation</u> as workers feel <u>more involved</u> in the production process.

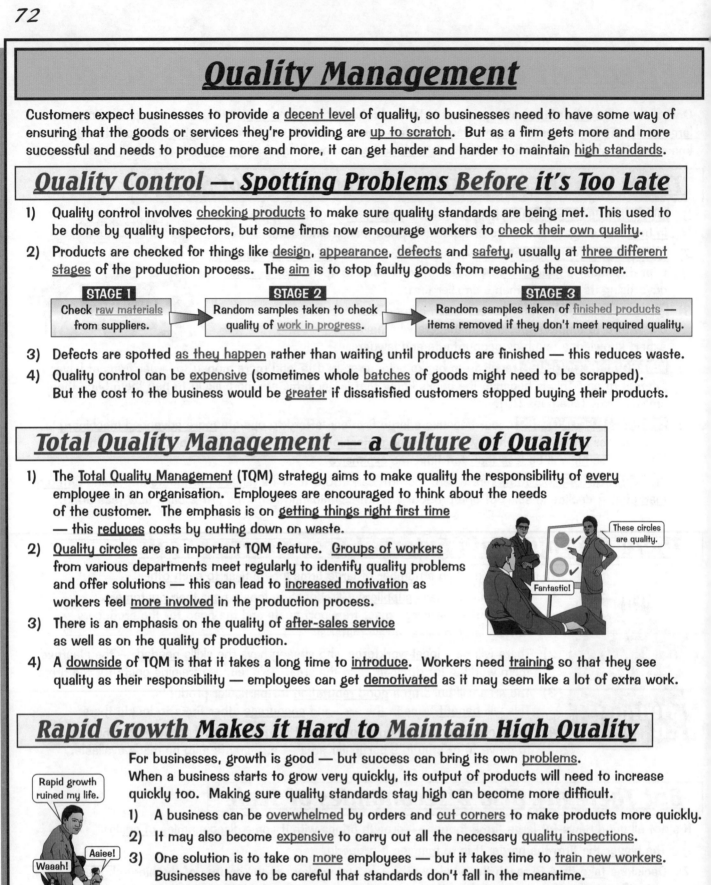

These circles are quality.

Fantastic!

3) There is an emphasis on the quality of <u>after-sales service</u> as well as on the quality of production.

4) A <u>downside</u> of TQM is that it takes a long time to <u>introduce</u>. Workers need <u>training</u> so that they see quality as their responsibility — employees can get <u>demotivated</u> as it may seem like a lot of extra work.

## Rapid Growth Makes it Hard to Maintain High Quality

Rapid growth ruined my life.

Waaah!   Aaiee!

For businesses, growth is good — but success can bring its own <u>problems</u>. When a business starts to grow very quickly, its output of products will need to increase quickly too. Making sure quality standards stay high can become more difficult.

1) A business can be <u>overwhelmed</u> by orders and <u>cut corners</u> to make products more quickly.

2) It may also become <u>expensive</u> to carry out all the necessary <u>quality inspections</u>.

3) One solution is to take on <u>more</u> employees — but it takes time to <u>train new workers</u>. Businesses have to be careful that standards don't fall in the meantime.

4) The business might <u>outsource</u> some tasks — that is, pay another company to do them. It can be <u>expensive</u> to outsource to a company that delivers <u>high</u> quality (but using a cheaper company can lead to a <u>fall</u> in quality).

## Quality circles — a well rounded idea...

The more words I type, the harder it gets to guarantee ~~kwality qualittie~~ <u>quality</u>. It's the same for growing businesses — making more products makes it harder to <u>maintain</u> quality. Ideas like <u>TQM</u> make quality important in <u>every part</u> of the business, but there's always the option to <u>outsource</u> if it all gets too much.

# Revision Summary for Section Ten

It's the end of Section Ten. Your business is growing, your labour is divided, your production is flowing. You've even got your head around economies of scale. Everything's looking good. But in exams, as in business, quality is important. If you're a bit shaky on the details, cracks are going to start showing in your answers. The questions on this page are a bit like quality control — you can spot any faults in your Business Studies knowledge before it's too late.

Sorry. I've been writing this Business Studies book for a long time — now I can't stop talking BS. What I mean is that answering these questions will be a good way of testing yourself on this section. I could have just said that in the first place, but I just couldn't stop going with the flow...

1) What does 'division of labour' mean?

2) Why does division of labour lead to more efficiency?

3) Describe three problems with division of labour.

4) Explain how specialisation makes firms interdependent.

5) Explain how a business may be able to introduce more efficient production methods as it grows.

6) What are the main features of flow production?

7) What type of products are usually manufactured using flow production? Why?

8) Draw a stock control chart for baked beans to show a maximum stock level of 300 cans, a minimum stock level of 100 cans and a re-order level of 200 cans.

9) What does lean production aim to eliminate?
   a) wasted raw materials     b) fatty foods     c) workers standing upright

10) Describe the differences between Just-in-Time (JIT) and Just-in-Case (JIC) stock control.

11) Explain one benefit and one problem of JIT.

12) Give three methods a firm might use to rationalise the business.

13) Explain the difference between internal and external economies of scale.

14) Give six examples of internal and four examples of external economies of scale.

15) What is meant by diseconomies of scale? Give two examples.

16) Why might poor quality control lead to a lot of waste?

17) What does TQM stand for? And what does TQM involve?

18) Give one advantage and one disadvantage of TQM.

19) Give three reasons why a growing business might find it hard to maintain high quality.

# What Examiners Want

Doing well in Business Studies is made a whole heap easier if you know what the examiners marking your <u>exam</u> (see p77) and your teacher marking your <u>controlled assessment</u> (see next page) are looking for.

## The Examiners are Looking for Three Types of Skills

There are basically three types of <u>skill</u> and <u>knowledge</u> that you need to show to get marks.
These go under the names of '<u>assessment objectives</u>'.

*AO1 = Assessment Objective 1 etc.*

### AO1 — Recall, Select and Communicate

- This assessment objective is all about... well... <u>recalling</u>, <u>selecting</u> and <u>communicating</u>.
    - You need to show that you've got a really good <u>understanding</u> of the facts, and that you can use appropriate <u>business terms</u>, e.g. sole trader, marketing mix, cash flow forecast.
    - And to get high marks in your controlled assessment, information needs to come from a <u>wide range</u> of sources and be <u>relevant</u> and <u>detailed</u>.

*You <u>don't</u> need to learn which skills come under which assessment objective. As long as you know what examiners are looking for, that's fine.*

### AO2 — Apply Skills, Knowledge and Understanding

- This objective is all about <u>applying</u> what you know to different situations.
- Make sure your answer is <u>relevant</u> to the situation that's been described.
- For example, an exam question might tell you about a <u>sole trader</u> who wants to buy a new piece of equipment, and ask you to suggest how they could raise the necessary finance. Here, you wouldn't want to suggest that the company issue more shares (since only a <u>limited company</u> can do this — <u>not</u> a <u>sole trader</u>).

- In your controlled assessment, you'll also get good marks if you plan and carry out <u>relevant</u> <u>field research</u> (see page 75).

### AO3 — Analyse and Evaluate Evidence

- This assessment objective is all about using <u>evidence</u> to make <u>judgements</u> and reach <u>conclusions</u>.
- For example, if you recommend that a business raise money using a mortgage rather than an overdraft, you need to explain <u>why</u>, using what you know about finance.

- Or if you've collected data from books or the internet for your controlled assessment, you need to <u>interpret</u> this data, and <u>use it</u> effectively to get high marks.
- Your ideas need to be <u>structured</u> in a logical way so that your arguments make <u>sense</u>.
- And your <u>spelling</u>, <u>punctuation</u> and <u>grammar</u> need to be lovely.

## My objective assessment?  I'm fed up of this BS...

Whatever happened to putting a right answer and getting a mark for it...  Anyway, it's good to know about how your work is going to be judged.  Doing well in assessment <u>isn't</u> just about knowing facts, it's about <u>communicating</u> to the examiner that you know the facts <u>so well</u> you can <u>apply</u> them in any situation.

# Controlled Assessment — Some Advice

You might think <u>controlled assessment</u> is a bit of a <u>drag</u>. I'd agree with you. But look on the bright side, it's better than a normal exam. But then most things in life are. Anyway, here's some info on <u>how to do well</u>...

## Controlled Assessment Tasks are Quite "Open"

1) Your controlled assessment is a <u>whole unit</u> in itself (Unit 3 — Investigating Business). And it's worth <u>25%</u> of your whole GCSE — that's a <u>lot</u>, so you need to take it seriously.

2) But you <u>don't</u> need to learn anything <u>extra</u> for it — it's based around the things you learned for Units 1 and 2 (so everything you need to know is covered in this book).

3) The controlled assessment task will involve writing some kind of <u>report</u> or <u>presentation</u>.

4) In some ways, the task will be quite <u>specific</u>. For example, you might have to:

> - <u>Produce</u> a business plan for a new business.
> - <u>Recommend</u> the best course of action for an existing business.
> - <u>Research</u> the methods a business uses to compete in its market, and decide which is most important.

*Ten people could answer the same question in ten completely different ways, but all get full marks.*

5) But there will always be <u>loads</u> of ways to approach the task. And you'll be able to include information from <u>loads</u> of different Business Studies topics.

6) The important thing is to do your own <u>research</u>, weigh up the <u>evidence</u>, and come to your own conclusions.

## First You'll Do Research, Then You'll Produce a Report

1) You won't be expected to write your report off the top of your head.

2) You'll be given <u>5-8 hours</u> (your teacher will tell you exactly) to <u>research and plan</u>. Your teacher will <u>supervise</u> you while you're doing your research, but you <u>can</u> ask for <u>help</u> if you really need it (though there are some things your teacher <u>can't</u> help you with — like analysing your research).

3) Once you've had your planning time you'll get <u>up to 3 hours</u> to <u>write it all up</u>. This will be much more like an <u>exam</u> — you <u>can't</u> ask for help during this bit.

## Make the Most of Your Research and Planning Time

1) Use your research time <u>efficiently</u>. Don't go mad — <u>quality</u> is more important than <u>quantity</u>.

2) Start off by thinking of the <u>big areas</u> you want to cover in your report. For example, if you've been asked to plan a business expansion, you could talk about <u>finance</u>, <u>recruitment</u>, <u>production</u>, <u>stakeholders</u>... and so on. (There might be some clues about this in the task blurb.)

3) You can then start to narrow things down a bit, and think of more <u>specific</u> issues you need to research. For example, you might decide you need to find out about the <u>different kinds</u> of finance available to a particular business in a particular area.

*<u>Plan</u> your research. <u>Don't</u> just browse the web and see what you come across.*

4) When you've got an overall plan you can start your <u>research</u>.

5) This might be <u>field research</u> — e.g. handing out <u>questionnaires</u>, or <u>interviewing</u> some local business people.

6) Or it might be <u>desk research</u>. For desk research, make sure you use varied sources of information (you'll get marks for doing this). Use books, newspapers, catalogues, price lists, the internet... whatever.

7) But stay <u>focused</u> — don't waste time researching stuff that you don't need. And don't spend five hours researching one thing — it won't leave enough time to cover the rest.

## Uncontrolled assessment — do what you like then hand it in...

I know, I know, there are a lot of words on this page. But look on the bright side (again), you don't actually have to learn them — they're here for your <u>information only</u>. Hurrah. Aren't bright sides awesome...

# Controlled Assessment — Some Advice

When you've done all your research, you'll need to <u>analyse</u> it, and then present your <u>findings</u>. If you like a bit of <u>detective work</u>, then controlled assessment will be right up your street.

## Analysis Means Understanding What Your Data's Saying

1) Analysis is all about organising and explaining a load of separate bits of information so that they make some kind of <u>overall sense</u> — so that you can describe everything as though it's a kind of '<u>story</u>'.

> Think about the bit near the end of an Hercule Poirot film when he gathers everyone in the library to tell them who the murderer is. He presents all the evidence, explains why it fits in with his version of events, and how it leads to his conclusion. This is a <u>bit</u> like what you need to do...

2) What you're really trying to do at this stage is <u>understand</u> what your research is telling you.

3) When you understand what your research is saying, you can start to <u>make decisions</u> about what you (or the business) should do next.

4) Always relate your research data to your <u>Business Studies knowledge</u> (this'll be good revision too).

5) You should always be able to <u>explain why</u> you've decided to <u>do this</u> or <u>recommend that</u> using your research. This means you're <u>backing up</u> your decisions or recommendations using <u>evidence</u>.

6) <u>Stick to the point</u> of the task — keep <u>re-reading</u> the question. It's incredibly easy to wander off the point unless you keep reminding yourself what the original question was.

## Your Report Needs to Be as Clear and Precise as Possible

1) Once you've got all your information, you'll need to find an <u>appropriate</u> way to <u>present</u> it.

2) Organising your data is vital. Decide which bits of research information you want to include, and put them into some kind of <u>logical order</u>, so the reader can also understand the 'story' your data is telling.

3) You also need to present information in the <u>clearest way</u> possible — for example, as text, in tables, as graphs... You need to choose the <u>best</u> method for your data.

| Sales of turnip juice in 2009 | | | | | |
|------|--------|-----|--------|-----|--------|
| Jan | 10,000 | May | 11,090 | Sep | 13,150 |
| Feb | 9,200 | Jun | 10,291 | Oct | 14,360 |
| Mar | 10,000 | Jul | 12,180 | Nov | 15,600 |
| Apr | 10,184 | Aug | 11,520 | Dec | 17,200 |

Not very clear — hard to see what's going on...

**Sales of turnip juice in 2009**

...but on this diagram, you can easily see that sales increased during 2009.

4) <u>Before</u> you start writing up your report, decide what your <u>conclusion</u> is going to be, then make sure that everything builds up to this in a logical way. And <u>link</u> bits of information together to make it as easy to follow as possible.

5) Examiners love <u>attention to detail</u>. If there are bits of information that don't fit in with an overall pattern — pick these out. If you can explain <u>why</u> they don't fit, then that's great. But even making a note of them without an explanation shows you're thinking.

6) Use plenty of appropriate <u>technical terms</u>. Take care with your <u>spelling</u>, <u>punctuation</u> and <u>grammar</u>. And leave yourself enough time to check that you've included <u>everything</u> that you were asked to.

7) One last thing... <u>don't plagiarise</u> — this means don't just find stuff on the internet, change a few words, and pretend <u>you</u> wrote it — that's <u>naughty</u>. But you can use <u>small</u> bits of other people's work as long as you say <u>where</u> you found it.

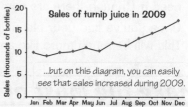

> <u>Always</u> keep a record of where your information came from. Write the name of the book or website where you found the information on a printout or photocopy — that'll make things easier later.

## Remember that Hercule Poirot bit and you'll be fine...

Hercule Poirot <u>doesn't</u> just <u>describe</u> his evidence... he works out what events must have happened to <u>create</u> that evidence. You need to do the same — try to understand <u>why</u> your data is as it is. Elementary.

# Know Your Exam

By now your brain should be full of Business Studies knowledge, ready to impress the examiners. These pages have info and tips on what to expect in the exams, so that you can ace them.

## There Are Two Exam Papers — Unit 1 and Unit 2

### Unit 1 — Setting Up a Business

- This is a 1-hour paper worth 60 marks.
- It'll test you on your knowledge of small businesses — the material that's covered in Section 1 to Section 5 of this book.

### Unit 2 — Growing as a Business

- This is also a 1-hour paper worth 60 marks.
- It's about growing businesses — all the stuff that's in Section 6 to Section 10 of this book.

There are no 'tick-the-box' questions for AQA. Make sure you're prepared for lots of writing.

1) In both papers there'll be three or four main questions, split into several parts.

2) Most questions will start with a business scenario.
The questions will be based around this scenario.

3) Some of the questions might ask you to interpret data (data-response questions).
All of the questions will ask for written answers — there aren't any "tick the box" questions.

## Pay Attention to Your Written Communication

You may think these next bits of advice are obvious. I don't care — read them anyway.
This stuff is worth banging on about.

### GIVING WRITTEN ANSWERS

1) There'll be a mixture of long-answer and short-answer questions.

2) Unless you're doing a calculation with numbers, you should write in complete sentences — you'll be given marks for your written communication (see page 74).

3) Always look at the marks available and the amount of space you've been given — use these as a guide to how long your answer should be. For example, if a question's worth 5 marks, it should take you about 5 minutes to answer, and you should aim to make (roughly) 5 valid points in your answer.

You won't get any marks for waffle.

### ANSWERING DATA-RESPONSE QUESTIONS

1) These questions give you information (or data) about a particular business — it might be a sales graph, a balance sheet, or even a newspaper article.

2) You need to apply your knowledge to the data — this might involve doing a calculation, making a recommendation based on the information, or something else entirely.

3) If you're asked for a calculation, you should show your working — even if you get the answer wrong, you might get marks for correct working.

4) Remember... always make sure your answer is relevant to the situation that's been described.

## All your questions about questions answered...

So, two exams, 1 hour each, answer in full sentences. Simple. Well... maybe 'simple' is a bit strong — they don't give these GCSEs away. But remembering some simple things can make your life that little bit easier.

# Command Words

All exam questions have a key "command" word that tells you what the examiner wants you to do.

## Some Words Test Your Knowledge...

Questions with these command words are testing what you know.

**Define or What is Meant By** — E.g. "What is meant by the term E-Commerce?" These questions are easy marks if you've learned all the definitions. You just have to know what the term means.

**Describe** — These usually need a bit more than "Define..." questions — e.g. "Describe the role of branding in a business." You'll have to make several points to answer this.

**State or Identify** — These words ask for a statement — you don't need to back it up with evidence.

**Give an Example** — Pretty obvious, really — use your knowledge to give an example of something. You might also be asked to find an example from a diagram or a set of figures.

## ...Some Words Test Your Knowledge and Understanding...

These command words test that you understand the concepts you've learned.
They're usually worth more marks, so they'll take longer to answer.

**Explain** — These questions are about giving reasons for things. You need to show that you understand the connection between things that happen in the world and the effects they have on businesses.

**Analyse** — This means "Examine in detail." Make sure you talk about the main features of the thing you're analysing. Then explain how or why these features work together to lead to the end result.

**Calculate** — Some questions ask for a bit of maths. Remember to show your working (have I said that before?).

## ...And Some Also Test Your Judgement

Examiners also like to test your ability to make judgements. To get top marks, you'll need to structure your answer — your ideas should flow in a logical way, and every point should lead towards your conclusion.

**Give Reasons for Your Answer** — If this phrase is in a question, you need to include lots of points and explain why they're relevant to your answer. Link your ideas together to build a balanced argument.

**Recommend   Discuss   Assess   Which is Most Likely/Appropriate   Evaluate**

These types of questions are all pretty similar. You'll be given some information about a particular business — you need to use this information and your knowledge of business studies in your answer.

- In business situations, there are usually advantages and disadvantages to think about — to get all the marks, you'll need to give both sides of the argument before coming to a conclusion.
- Before you get started on your answer, make sure you've read the whole question carefully and you've understood what you're being asked to do. You'll lose marks if you take the wrong approach.

**Do you think** — When examiners ask you what you think, they're not just asking for an opinion off the top of your head. You need to back up your point of view with evidence and a structured argument.

## Sick of revision yet? Give reasons for your answer...

Command words aren't set in stone — the same word might be used in slightly different ways in different questions. But if you read the whole question, it should be clear what you need to do to get the marks.

# Mark Schemes

Mark schemes explain <u>exactly</u> what examiners <u>can</u> give marks for, and what they <u>can't</u> — so it's useful to know the kinds of things they have on them. And because I'm all about being useful, here's an <u>example</u>. Smashing.

## Mark Schemes Tell the Examiner How to Mark Answers

**Example Question:** Alice is planning to open a new vegetarian café in Manchester. Assess the importance of good customer service in increasing the competitive advantage of Alice's café. *(9 marks)*

The command word here is <u>assess</u> so you'll need to make a <u>judgement</u>... and <u>support</u> it with <u>evidence</u>. The mark scheme for this question is split into <u>two parts</u> — these show what the <u>9 marks</u> available are given for.

*The first part of the mark scheme shows how AO1 and AO2 marks are given, while the second part is for AO3 (see p74).*

**PART 1** (Assessment Objective being marked)

| AO | Description of Answer | Marks |
|---|---|---|
| AO1 | No valid response. | 0 |
| | The answer states relevant point(s). | 1 |
| AO2 | The answer provides explanation of point(s). | 2 |

1) You'd get 1 mark for just <u>stating a point</u> about how important customer service is in increasing the café's competitive advantage.

2) You'd get a second mark for <u>explaining</u> the point.

**PART 2**

| AO | Description of Answer | Marks |
|---|---|---|
| AO3 | The answer gives an unsupported judgement. Written communication is simplistic, and very few technical terms are correctly used. | 1-2 |
| | The answer gives a judgement with some support and justification. Ideas are communicated with some structure and use of technical terms (though some may be used incorrectly). | 3-5 |
| | Candidate offers judgement with justification. Ideas are communicated with a clear structure and correct use of technical terms. | 6-7 |

3) If you think customer service is important to the competitiveness of Alice's café, but <u>don't say why</u> you think this, you'll get 1 or 2 marks out of a possible 7.

4) If you say how important you think it is, and give <u>reasons</u> to back it up, throwing in some <u>technical terms</u> along the way, you can get up to 5 marks.

5) The more <u>evidence</u> you give to <u>support</u> your judgement, the better the <u>links</u> between your points, and the more <u>relevant technical terms</u> you use, the more marks you'll get.

6) To get 6 or 7 marks you'd need to give a <u>well written</u> argument to explain your opinion, with a sensible <u>structure</u> to show how your ideas relate to each other. You'll also score well if you can judge <u>which</u> features of customer service are <u>most likely</u> to affect the café's competitive advantage.

7) Your <u>writing</u> needs to be clear and accurate to get these marks — so watch your <u>spelling</u>, <u>grammar</u> and <u>punctuation</u>. Here's an example of the sort of thing you could write for <u>part</u> of your answer:

> Training staff to provide good service can be expensive, and these costs may lead to higher prices. However, people are often prepared to pay slightly higher prices for good service (and are often put off by poor service). As long as prices do not become too high, Alice may be able to increase customer loyalty by offering a better customer experience than competing cafés, meaning that customers will choose to return to Alice's café.

8) You've been asked to <u>assess</u> the situation, so you'll need to come to a <u>conclusion</u>. For example:

> Overall, the benefits of customer service should outweigh the costs to the business (and the potential cost of not offering a decent level of service could be very high indeed if it puts customers off). Offering a high level of customer service could be a way for Alice to differentiate her café from competitors', and achieve a crucial competitive advantage.

9) Remember there's <u>no right answer</u> — just make sure you back up your opinion with sensible reasons.

## These schemes are useful — you mark my words...

Remember to always look at the <u>number of marks</u> available for a question — the more marks available, the more detailed your answer will need to be. It's an obvious point, but it's easy to forget in a stressful exam.

# Sample Exam Questions

Here's a sample of the type of question you're likely to find in your exam.

## Many Exam Questions are Based on a Particular Scenario

1. Nasir is the manager of TotalTees Ltd — a small, struggling company manufacturing T-shirts.

*Many questions start with some background information about a business — read it carefully.*

a) Last year's trading, profit and loss account for TotalTees Ltd is shown on the right.

Calculate last year's gross profit margin. Show all of your working clearly. *(2 marks)*

gross profit margin = gross profit ÷ sales (turnover)
= 24,000 ÷ 44,000
= 0.55 (or 55%)

| Trading, Profit and Loss Account TotalTees Ltd Year ending 31st March 2008 | £000 | £000 |
|---|---|---|
| Turnover | | 44 |
| Cost of sales: | | |
| Opening stock | 4 | |
| Purchases | 23 | |
| | 27 | |
| Minus closing stock | (7) | |
| Cost of sales = | | (20) |
| Gross profit = | | 24 |

A bit of maths here — you'd get 2 marks for the correct answer.

But if you get the answer wrong, you can still get 1 mark for using the correct method — so make sure you show your working. (You'd be given the formula if this were a real exam — but make sure you know how to use it.)

b) Nasir believes that some of TotalTees' products are in the decline phase of their life cycle.

Identify one extension strategy that the company could use. *(1 mark)*

They could reduce the prices of those products.

For part b), you're only asked to identify the extension strategy — you don't need to explain how it works.

c) Nasir wants to increase the motivation of workers on the factory's production line. One option is to give workers a 5% increase in their wages.

The workers currently earn £7.00 per hour. Calculate what their hourly wage would be after the 5% pay rise. Show your working. *(2 marks)*

1% of £7 = 7 ÷ 100 = £0.07. So 5% of £7 = 0.07 × 5 = £0.35

Wage after pay rise = £7.00 + £0.35 = £7.35 per hour.

Another bit of maths — another 2 marks for the correct answer.

As always, show your working. If you get the wrong answer, you can still get 1 mark for your working.

d) Nasir is also considering using a non-financial motivation method.

i) Identify and explain one example of a non-financial method of motivation that the firm could use. *(2 marks)*

Job rotation — this is where workers regularly change between jobs in the factory. This increases motivation by making the work more varied and less boring.

The firm needs to choose between a 5% wage increase or the non-financial method you identified in part (i).

ii) Which method do you think would be most appropriate for motivating workers at the firm? Give reasons for your answer. *(3 marks)*

Factory workers are likely to work mainly for money, so would be motivated by a pay rise. On the other hand, job rotation would be cheaper for the company and this is the method I think is more appropriate here. If the company is already struggling, then increasing costs with a pay rise might make the situation worse.

Here you have to explain how the method you've chosen works and why it might help to motivate staff.

You'd get 1 mark for identifying an appropriate method, and 1 mark for explaining it correctly.

Part (ii) asks for a judgement, so weigh up both sides of the argument in your answer. And if you can use some technical terms in your answer, then so much the better.

## Let's get down to Business...

For each question in the exam, look at the command words and the number of marks. Remember that longer questions are usually testing your judgement as well as your knowledge, so support your ideas with evidence.

# Sample Exam Questions

I know I'm banging on a bit, but the key to any question is that command word.
Make sure you understand it before you start writing. It's all about doing as you're told.

## Some Questions Need Long, Structured Answers

1. Sarah is a young clothes designer, and is starting her own business designing, manufacturing and selling her own ranges of fashionwear. Sarah is considering only direct channels of distribution.

a) What is a direct channel of distribution? *(2 marks)*

*A direct channel of distribution means that the manufacturer sells their goods directly to the customer without involving any intermediaries (such as retailers or wholesalers).*

> This part is just testing what you know. Not many marks available, so just write down the definition and move on...

b) Sarah decides to sell her goods either over the internet or to open her own shop. Describe how the potential market for her products might be affected by her choice. *(3 marks)*

*If Sarah chooses to open a shop, her market will be limited to customers in the nearby area. But if she chooses to sell her clothes over the internet, she will in theory be able to target a much wider (even international) market. However, a lot of people prefer to visit a real shop to try on clothes, so Sarah may be restricting her potential market if she uses just the internet. There are also some people without access to the internet that Sarah will not be able to reach.*

> Now you get to add a bit more detail, and explain some of Sarah's likely considerations.
>
> To answer this question, you need to use your Business Studies knowledge, but you should make sure your explanations all relate to Sarah's business.

c) Describe the value of market research to an entrepreneur like Sarah. Recommend some types of market research that she could carry out. *(9 marks)*

*Market research is absolutely vital to someone starting up a new business. Market-driven firms tend to be more successful than product-driven ones, so finding out about customers' likes and dislikes, how much they would be prepared to pay for certain items, and where they prefer to buy, could be the difference between Sarah's business succeeding and failing.*

*Sarah should find out the types and prices of products that are popular and unpopular, where customers currently shop, and whether they would consider shopping for clothes over the internet. Desk research is relatively cheap, so Sarah should use this as much as she can. For example, she might be able to find out some useful information from market research reports, or magazine and internet articles (e.g. about popular fashions, or how many people buy clothes over the internet). But to find some types of information, Sarah may need to use field research. For example, if she has potential locations for a shop in mind, she should visit those areas and interview people to see the level of interest in her idea for a new shop, as well as researching the level of local competition.*

> There are lots of marks available here (and lots of space to write your answer)...
>
> The first command word here is 'describe', so you're going to have to make at least a couple of points about the value of market research.
>
> Then you've got to 'recommend' some (i.e. more than one) market research activities. Think of the "4 Marketing P's" — this is what Sarah will want info about. Then think of ways Sarah might find that info out. She'd probably prefer to find out as much as she can using desk research, but you might recommend doing some field research too.

## And that, as they say, is that...

That's the end of the book. By now, you should have a head crammed full of Business Studies knowledge (probably so full that even now facts are dripping out your ears), and you should know exactly what your assessment will involve, and how to go about doing it. So what are you waiting for... go get that GCSE...

# Index

# *Index*

# Index